FOR THE SUMMER BETWEEN GRADES
3–4

SUMMER SUCCESS

McGraw-Hill Children's Publishing
Columbus, Ohio

 **Children's Publishing**

Copyright © 2003 McGraw-Hill Children's Publishing. Published by American Education Publishing, an imprint of McGraw-Hill Children's Publishing, a Division of The McGraw-Hill Companies.

Printed in the United States of America. All rights reserved. Except as permitted under the United States Copyright Act, no part of this publication may be reproduced or distributed in any form or by any means, or stored in a database or retrieval system, without prior written permission from the publisher, unless otherwise indicated.

Send all inquiries to:
McGraw-Hill Children's Publishing
8787 Orion Place
Columbus, OH 43240-4027

ISBN 1-57768-533-4

1 2 3 4 5 6 7 8 9 10 CJK 08 07 06 05 04 03

Table of Contents

Summer Success Recommended Reading 4
Number Sense 5-8
Number Operations 9-20
Statistics 21
Algebra 22
Computation 23-28
Measurement 29-33
Geometry 34-41
Logical Thinking 42-43
Probability 44
Vocabulary Strategies 45-47
Language Conventions 48-55
Mechanics Conventions 56-57
Parts of Speech 58-64
Reading Strategies 65-71
Reading for Different Purposes 72-74
Literature Forms 75
Writing Strategies 76-80
Using Reference Materials 81-83
Glossary 84-85
Answer Key 86-94
Skills Checklist 95-96

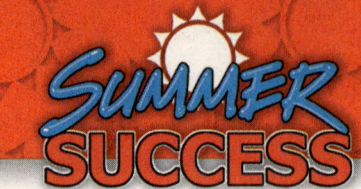

Recommended Summer Reading Grades 3-4

Art and Civilization Series: Ancient Rome; Medieval Times; Prehistory	McGraw-Hill Children's Publishing
The Bad Beginning	Lemony Snicket
Because of Winn-Dixi	Kate Dicamillo
Cam Jansen and the Mystery of the Television Dog	David Adler
The Castle in the Attic	Elizabeth Winthrop
Charlie and the Chocolate Factory; Roald Dahl's Revolting Rhymes	Roald Dahl
Charlotte's Web; Stuart Little	E.B. White
Encyclopedia Brown Takes the Cake	Donald J. Sobol
Grasshopper Summer	Ann Turner
Gray Feather and the Big Dog	Cesar Vidal
Heartlight	T.A. Barron
How to Eat Fried Worms	Thomas Rockwell
The Incredible Journey to the Mummy's Tomb	Nicholas Harris
Insectlopedia: Poems and Paintings	Douglas Florian
It's Raining Pigs and Noodles	Jack Prelutsky
Lunch Box Mail and Other Poems	Jenny Whitehead
Magic School Bus: Inside a Hurricane	Joanna Cole
Meet Kaya	Janet Shaw
The Mouse and the Motorcycle	Beverly Cleary
Myth Series: Egyptian; Greek; Roman; Celtic	McGraw-Hill Children's Publishing
My America: A Poetry Atlas of the U.S.	Lee Bennett Hopkins
The Night Journey	Kathryn Lasky
On the Far Side of the Mountain	Jean Craighead George
Raiders and Traders; Emperors and Gladiators; Athletes and Actors	Anita Ganeri
Ramona's World; Ramona and Her Father	Judy Blume
The Rough Face Girl	Rafe Martin
Sarah Plain and Tall	Patricia MacLachlan
Sideways Stories from Wayside School	Louis Sachar
So You Want to be President?	Judith St. George
The Stinky Cheeseman and Other Fairly Stupid Tales	Jon Scieszka
Tales of a Fourth Grade Nothing	Judy Blume
Valdores	Patricia Peterson

Write That Number

Directions: Write the numeral form for each number.

Example: three hundred forty-two = 342

1. six hundred fifty thousand, two hundred twenty-five _____

2. nine hundred ninety-nine thousand, nine hundred ninety-nine _____

3. one hundred six thousand, four hundred thirty-seven _____

4. three hundred fifty-six thousand, two hundred two _____

5. Write the number that is two more than 356,909. _____

6. Write the number that is five less than 448,394. _____

7. Write the number that is ten more than 285,634. _____

8. Write the number that is ten less than 395,025. _____

Directions: Write the following numbers in word form.

9. 3,208 _____

10. 13,656 _____

5

Name _____

Can You Place It?

The **place value** of a digit, or numeral, is shown by where it is in the number. For example, in the number 1,234, 1 has the place value of thousands, 2 is hundreds, 3 is tens, and 4 is ones.

Hundred Thousands	Ten Thousands	Thousands	Hundreds	Tens	Ones
9	4	3	8	5	2

943,852

Directions: Match the numbers in Column A with the words in Column B. The first one is done for you.

A	B
62,453	two hundred thousand
7,641	three thousand
486,113	four hundred thousand
11,277	eight hundreds
813,463	seven tens
594,483	five ones
254,089	six hundreds
79,841	nine ten thousands
27,115	five tens

Name _____

Greater Than / Less Than

When numbers are compared, one can be:
- **greater than**   >
- **less than**   <
- **or equal to**   =   another number

Directions: Place the correct symbol between each set of numbers.

1.	45	26	**5.**	379	979	**9.**	5,760	2,899
2.	243	456	**6.**	2,578	989	**10.**	11	9
3.	1,354	2,678	**7.**	57	38	**11.**	71	211
4.	24	24	**8.**	194	59	**12.**	4,000	4,005

Chart your answers. Make one talley each time you use a symbol.

>	
<	
=	

Answer the questions. Circle the correct answer.

Which has the fewest?   >,   <,   or   =

Which has the most?   >,   <,   or   =

Name _____

Round Them Up!

You can estimate by rounding a number up or down. If the tens number is 5 or greater, "round up" to the nearest hundred. If the tens number is 4 or less, the hundreds number remains the same.

Remember to look at the number directly to the right of the place you are rounding to.

Example:

2**3**0 round <u>down</u> to 200

4**7**0 round <u>up</u> to 500

1**5**0 round <u>up</u> to 200

7**3**2 round <u>down</u> to 700

Directions: Round the following numbers to the nearest hundred. Fill in the bubble next to the correct answer.

1. 456
   ○ 400
   ○ 500

2. 340
   ○ 300
   ○ 400

3. 867
   ○ 800
   ○ 900

4. 686
   ○ 600
   ○ 700

5. 770
   ○ 700
   ○ 800

6. 120
   ○ 100
   ○ 200

7. 923
   ○ 900
   ○ 1000

8. 550
   ○ 500
   ○ 600

9. 231
   ○ 200
   ○ 300

10. 492
    ○ 400
    ○ 500

Name _____

Leafy Addition

Directions: Add, then color according to the code.

Code:

green — 79   orange — 35   red — 78
yellow — 87   purple — 56   brown — 94

57
+ 21

34
+ 22

23
+ 12

35
+ 52

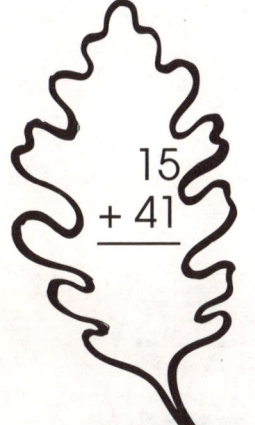
15
+ 41

62
+ 32

20
+ 74

34
+ 44

56
+ 23

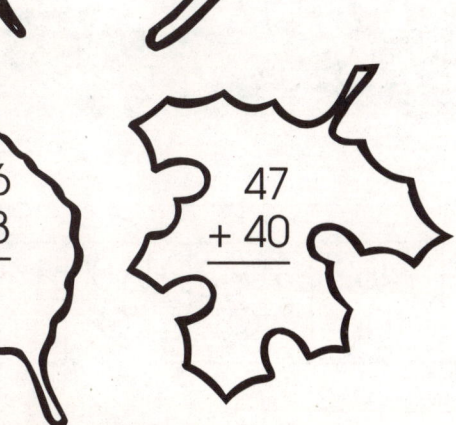
47
+ 40

27
+ 8

63
+ 16

Name _____

Adding-It-Up Puzzle

Sometimes numbers have to be carried to the next column to complete an operation. This is called **regrouping**.

Add the ones. Regroup.	Add the tens. Regroup.	Add the hundreds. Regroup.	Add the thousands. Regroup.
1 7,465 +4,978 3	11 7,465 +4,978 43	1 1 1 7,465 +4,978 443	1 1 1 7,465 +4,978 12,443

Directions: Add using regrouping. Then use the code to discover the name of a United States president.

```
  348      642      386      184
 +752     +277     +787     +875


  578      653      653      946
 +874     +768     +359     +239


  393      199      721
 +257     +843     +679
```

____ . ____ ____ ____ ____ ____ ____ ____ ____ ____

1012	1173	1059	1421	919	650	1452	1042	1100	1400	1185
N	A	S	I	W	T	H	O	G	N	G

10

Name _____

Scoreboard Subtraction

Subtraction means "taking away" or subtracting one number from another to find the difference. For example, 10 - 3 = 7. To regroup is to use one ten to form ten ones, one 100 to form ten tens and so on.

Directions: Study the example. Subtract using regrouping.

Example:

```
 32  =   2 tens  +  12 ones
-13  =   1 ten   +   3 ones
 19  =   1 ten   +   9 ones
```

```
  33        86        92        71
 -28       -59       -37       -48
```

```
  63        45        31        55
 -47       -18       -22       -39
```

82 - 69 = ____   73 - 36 = ____

The Yankees won 85 games.
The Cubs won 69 games.
How many more games
did the Yankees win? _____

11

Fancy Flower Subtraction

Directions: **Regrouping** for subtraction is the opposite of regrouping for addition. Study the example. Subtract using regrouping. Then use the code to color the flowers.

Example:

           Steps:

647   1. Subtract ones.

−453   2. Subtract tens. Five tens cannot be subtracted from 4 tens.

194   3. Regroup tens by regrouping 6 hundreds (5 hundreds + 10 tens).

           4. Add the 10 tens to the four tens.

           5. Subtract 5 tens from 14 tens.

           6. Subtract the hundreds.

If the answer has:
1 one, color it red;
8 ones, color it pink;
5 ones, color it yellow.

Name _____

Problem Solving at the Fair

Directions: Read and solve each problem. Fill in the bubble next to the correct answer.

1. The clown started the day with 200 balloons. He gave away 128 of them. Some broke. At the end of the day he had 18 balloons left. How many of the balloons broke?
   ○ 18
   ○ 54
   ○ 72

2. On Monday, there were 925 tickets sold to adults and 1,412 tickets sold to children. How many more children attended the fair than adults?
   ○ 487
   ○ 513
   ○ 2,337

3. At one game booth, prizes were given out for scoring 500 points in three attempts. Sally scored 178 points on her first attempt, 149 points on her second attempt and 233 points on her third attempt. Did Sally win a prize?
   ○ no
   ○ yes

4. The prize-winning steer weighed 2,348 pounds. The runner-up steer weighed 2,179 pounds. How much more did the prize steer weigh?
   ○ 169 lbs.
   ○ 231 lbs.
   ○ 527 lbs.

Name _____

Multiplication Race

Multiplication means taking a number and adding it to itself a certain number of times.

Directions: Time yourself as you multiply. How quickly can you complete this page?

```
  3      8      1      1      3      0
 x2     x7     x0     x6     x4     x4


  4      4      2      9      9      5
 x1     x4     x5     x3     x9     x3


  0      2      9      8      7      4
 x8     x6     x6     x5     x3     x2


  3      2      4      1      0      3
 x5     x0     x6     x3     x0     x3
```

Name _____

Amazing Arms

What will happen to a starfish that loses an arm? To find out, solve the following problems and write the matching letter above the answer at the bottom of the page.

O. 2,893　　W. 1,763　　W. 7,665
  × 4　　　　× 3　　　　× 5

A. 1,935　　W. 3,097　　E. 2,929
  × 6　　　　× 3　　　　× 4

G. 6,366　　T. 7,821　　L. 6,283　　I. 5,257　　R. 3,019
  × 5　　　　× 8　　　　× 7　　　　× 3　　　　× 6

　　　　　　　　　　　　N. 2,908　　I. 6,507　　N. 5,527
　　　　　　　　　　　　 × 7　　　　× 8　　　　× 2

　　　　　　　　　　　　L. 6,626　　O. 7,219　　E. 3,406
　　　　　　　　　　　　 × 3　　　　× 9　　　　× 6

___ ___
52,056 62,568

___ ___ ___ ___ ___ ___ ___ ___
5,289 15,771 43,981 19,878 31,830 18,114 64,971 9,291

___ ___ ___ ___ ___ ___ ___ !
11,610 20,356 20,436 38,325 11,572 11,054 11,716

15

Name _____

Multiplication Puzzles With Regrouping

Example:

Steps:

Multiply by the ones. Carry numbers as needed.	Multiply by the tens. Carry numbers as needed. Put a zero in the ones place.	Add.
5 3 6,074 × 38 48,592	2 1 1 6,074 × 38 48,592 182,220	6,074 × 38 48,592 +182,220 230,812

Directions: Multiply along each diagonal of the square. Write the answer in the oval.

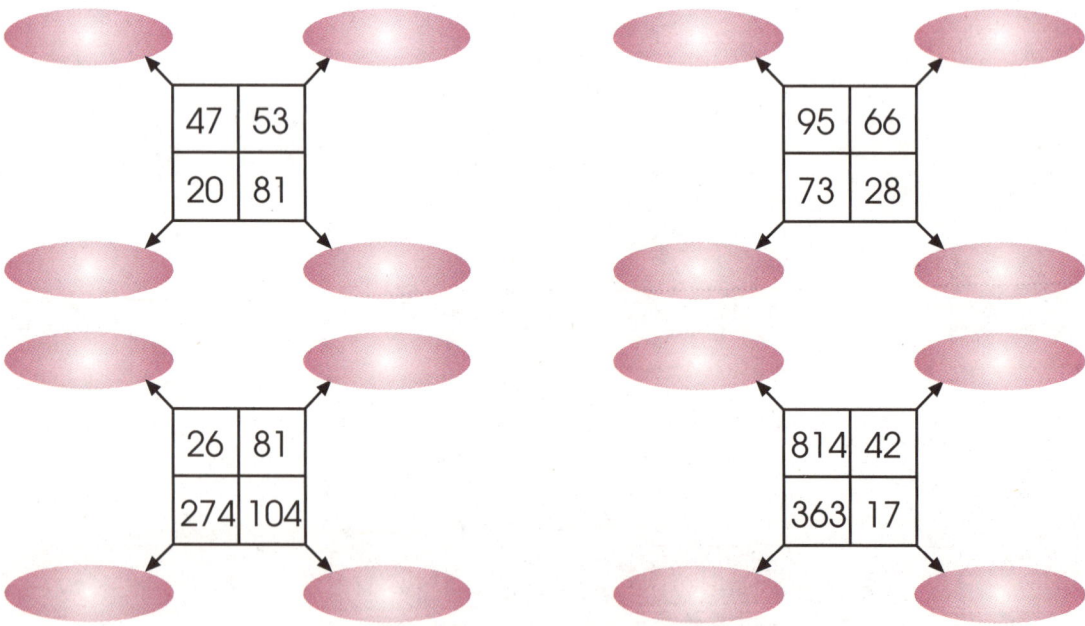

What is the pattern of the answers on opposite corners? Why is that so?

_____

16

Name _____

Match the Sail

Division shows how many times one number contains another.

Directions: Divide. Draw a line from the boat to the sail with the correct answer. The first one has been done for you.

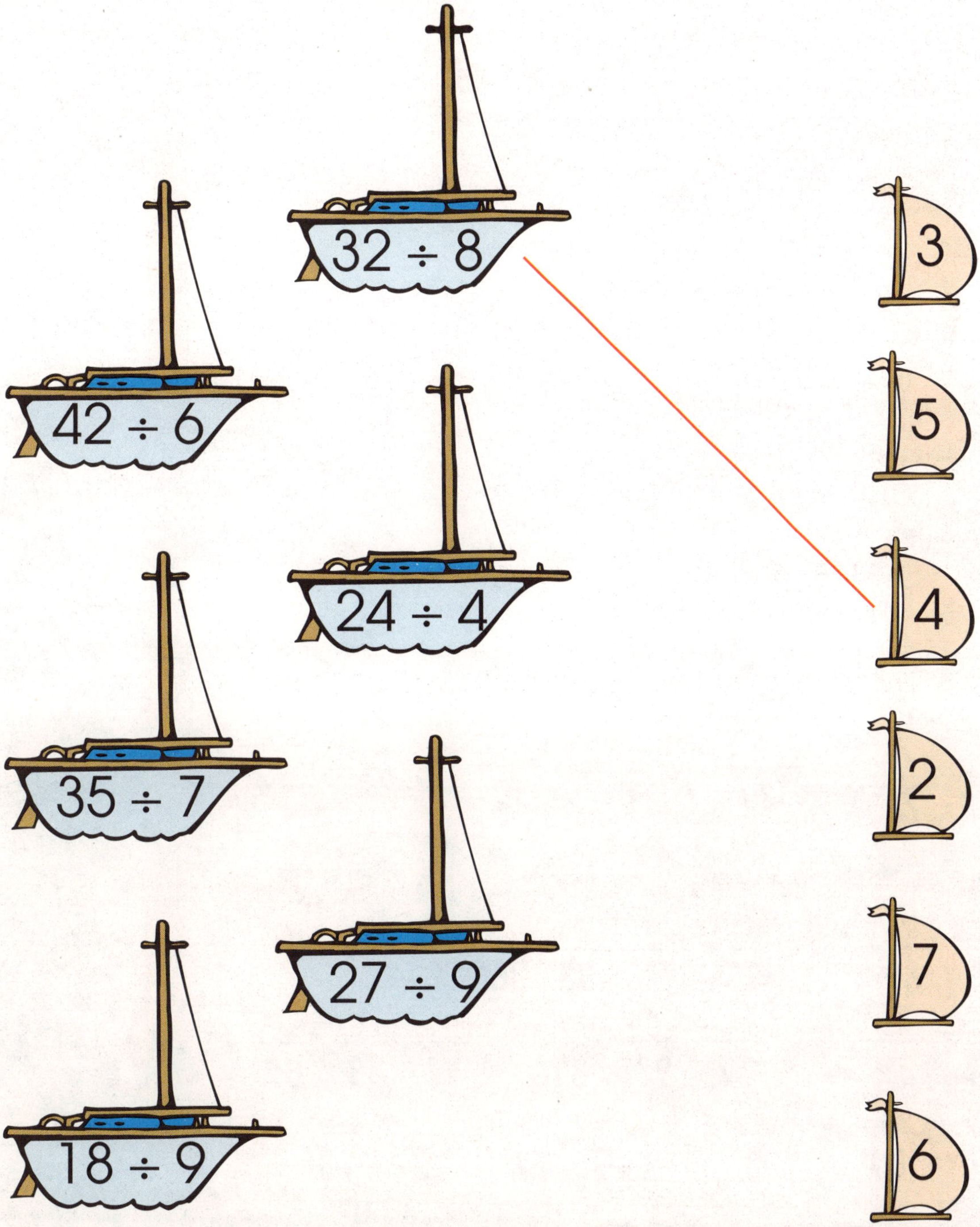

- $32 \div 8$
- $42 \div 6$
- $24 \div 4$
- $35 \div 7$
- $27 \div 9$
- $18 \div 9$

Sails: 3, 5, 4, 2, 7, 6

17

Name _____

Division Drop In

Directions: What does "dropping in" mean to a skateboarder? To find out, solve each division problem. Then, write the matching letter above the answer below.

O = 4)356

T = 6)246

T = 3)525

P = 9)684

R = 6)930

A = 4)392

H = 3)291

P = 8)496

T = 3)201

F = 6)294

E = 7)448

S = 5)375

T = 9)648

T = 6)192

R = 2)730

A = 5)385

M = 4)292

175	89		75	41	98	365	67	
77	32		72	97	64		41	89	62
89	49	98		155	77		73	76	

18

On the Road

The Olympics are held in a different international city every time. All athletes must travel to play or compete.

Directions: Your bags are packed with division problems. Solve these problems.

Steps for division:
1. Divide.
2. Multiply.
3. Subtract.
4. Bring down.
5. Go back to step 1 or add the remainder.

Example:

$$4\overline{)19} \quad \begin{array}{r} 4\text{R}3 \\ -16 \\ \hline 3 \end{array}$$

$8\overline{)55}$

$5\overline{)29}$

$8\overline{)30}$

$9\overline{)63}$

$3\overline{)7}$

$7\overline{)34}$

$4\overline{)24}$

$6\overline{)53}$

$2\overline{)11}$ $7\overline{)40}$ $6\overline{)22}$ $2\overline{)12}$ $8\overline{)44}$ $5\overline{)33}$ $3\overline{)17}$

Problem Solving in the Garden

Directions: Read and solve each problem using either multiplication or division.

Jeff and Terry are planting a garden. They plant 3 rows of green beans with 8 plants in each row. How many green bean plants are there in the garden? _____

There are 45 tomato plants in the garden. There are 5 rows of them. How many tomato plants are in each row? _____

The children have 12 plants each of lettuce, broccoli, and spinach. How many plants are there in all? _____

Jeff planted 3 times as many cucumber plants as Terry. He planted 15 of them. How many did Terry plant? _____

Terry planted 12 pepper plants. He planted twice as many green pepper plants as red pepper plants. How many green pepper plants are there? _____

How many red pepper plants? _____

Name _____

Using a Calculator

Here are some examples of how to enter problems into a calculator.

3 2 8 + 1 9 6 = 524

5 4 + 7 8 + 3 8 + 1 2 3 = 293

9 8 3 − 2 3 1 = 752

3 2 × 5 4 = 1,728

1 , 8 9 2 ÷ 4 = 473

Directions: Use a calculator to solve.

404,992 ÷ 452 = _____

35 x 28 x 81 x 10 = _____

4,906 x 659 = _____

239,476 − 20,395 = _____

436,284 + 1,293,058 = _____

33,482 x 2,338 = _____

498 + 298 + 3,904 + 637 + 1,293 = _____

284 x 47 + 1,842 = _____

45,337 − 28,493 = _____

63,856 + 283,447 − 143,396 = _____

2,004 x 742 = _____

2,184,396 ÷ 4 + 5,693 = _____

763,100 ÷ 325 = _____

493 x 329 − 32,058 = _____

Does anything happen if you divide 1,024 ÷ 2 and hit the = key over and over? If so, what? _____

21

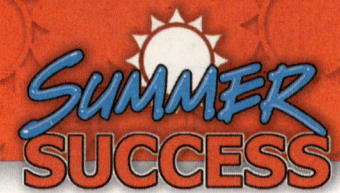

The Order of Things

When you solve a problem that involves more than one operation, this is the order to follow, known as the **Order of Operations**:

( ) Parentheses first
x Multiplication
÷ Division
+ Addition
− Subtraction

Example:
2 + (3 x 5) - 2 = 15
2 + 15 - 2 = 15
17 - 2 = 15

Directions: Solve the problems using the correct order of operations or use +, −, x, and ÷ to complete the problems so the number sentence is true.

(5 - 3) + 4 x 7 = ____

9 ____ 3 ____ 9 = 3

(8 ____ 2) ____ 4 = 8

1 + 2 x 3 + 4 = ____

Associative Property of Multiplication:

(a x b) x c = a x (b x c)

Commutative Property of Multiplication:

a x b = b x a

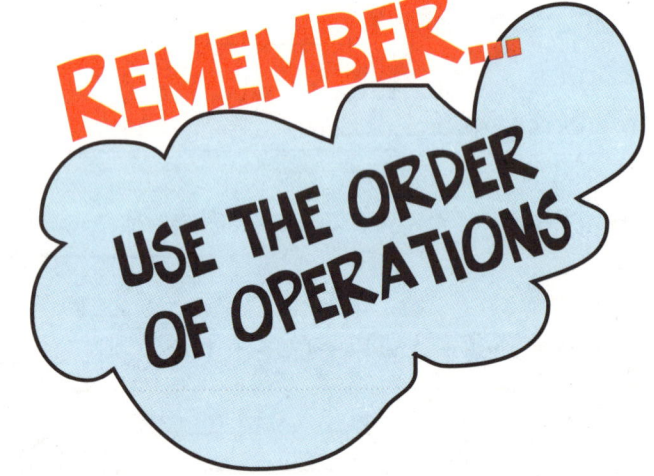

Directions: Fill in the blanks so that the number sentence is true.

(4 x 2) x 2 = ____ x (2 x ____)

2 x 11 = ____ x ____

6 x ____ = 7 x 6

(9 x 2) x ____ = ____ x (____ x 1)

22

Name _____

Flourishing Fractions

The bottom number in a fraction, telling the number of parts in the whole, is called a **denominator**. The **numerator** is the top part of a fraction that shows the number of parts out of the whole.

When adding fractions with the same denominator, the denominator stays the same. Add only the numerators.

Example: numerator $\frac{1}{8}$ + $\frac{2}{8}$ = $\frac{3}{8}$
denominator

Directions: Add the fractions on the flowers. Begin in the center of each flower and add each petal. The first one is done for you.

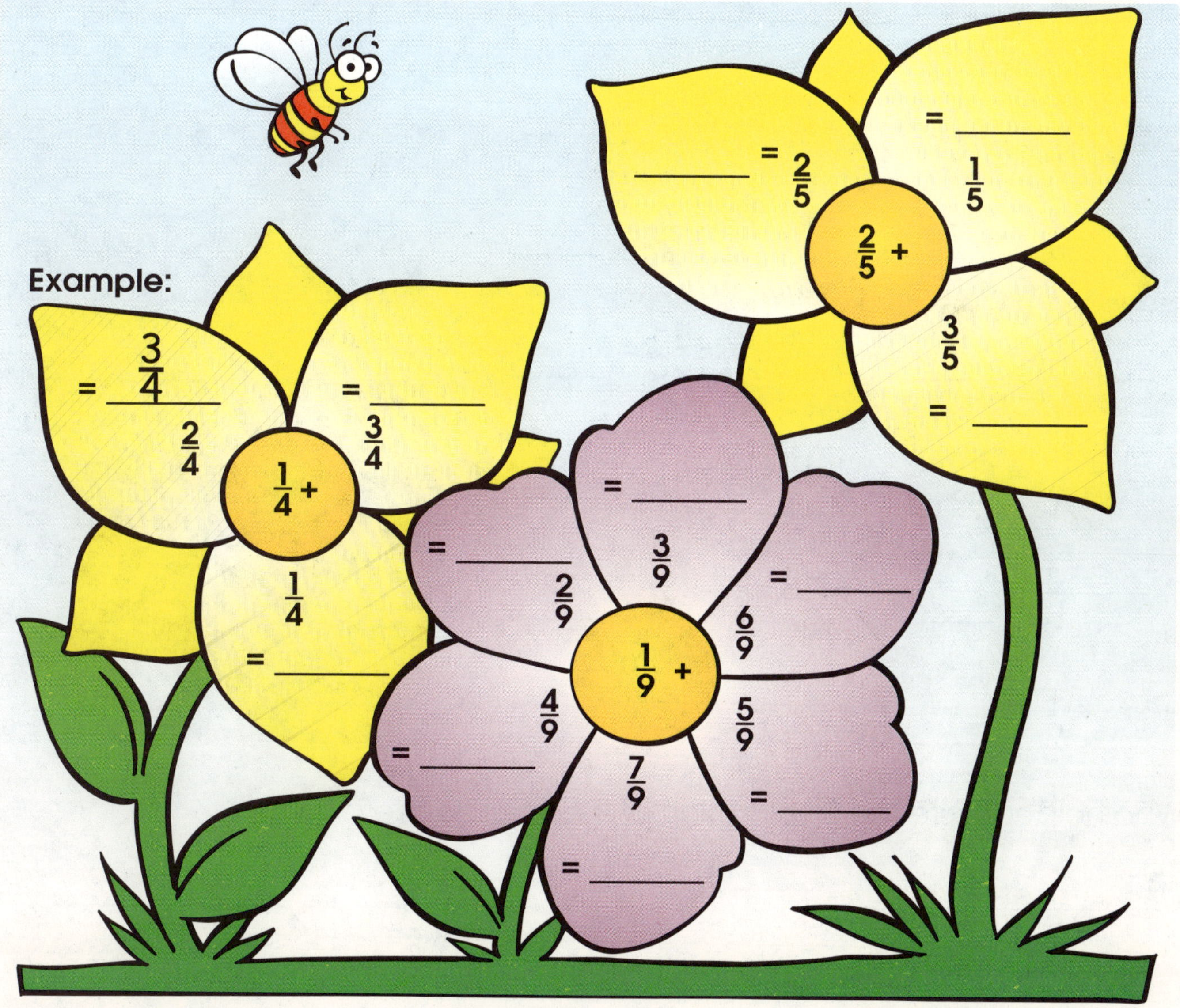

Example:

Falling Fractions

When subtracting fractions with the same denominator, the denominator stays the same. Subtract only the numerators.

Directions: Solve the problems, working from left to right. As you find each answer, copy the letter from the key into the numbered blanks. The answer is the name of a famous American. The first one is done for you.

1. $\frac{3}{8} - \frac{2}{8} = \underline{\frac{1}{8}}$
2. $\frac{2}{4} - \frac{1}{4} = \underline{}$
3. $\frac{5}{9} - \frac{3}{9} = \underline{}$
4. $\frac{2}{3} - \frac{1}{3} = \underline{}$
5. $\frac{8}{12} - \frac{7}{12} = \underline{}$
6. $\frac{4}{5} - \frac{1}{5} = \underline{}$
7. $\frac{6}{12} - \frac{3}{12} = \underline{}$
8. $\frac{4}{9} - \frac{1}{9} = \underline{}$
9. $\frac{11}{12} - \frac{7}{12} = \underline{}$
10. $\frac{7}{8} - \frac{3}{8} = \underline{}$
11. $\frac{4}{7} - \frac{2}{7} = \underline{}$
12. $\frac{14}{16} - \frac{7}{16} = \underline{}$
13. $\frac{18}{20} - \frac{13}{20} = \underline{}$
14. $\frac{13}{15} - \frac{2}{15} = \underline{}$
15. $\frac{5}{6} - \frac{3}{6} = \underline{}$

T	$\frac{1}{8}$	P	$\frac{5}{24}$	H	$\frac{1}{4}$
F	$\frac{4}{12}$	E	$\frac{2}{7}$	J	$\frac{3}{12}$
E	$\frac{3}{9}$	O	$\frac{2}{9}$	F	$\frac{4}{8}$
R	$\frac{7}{16}$	O	$\frac{2}{8}$	Y	$\frac{8}{20}$
Q	$\frac{1}{32}$	M	$\frac{1}{3}$	S	$\frac{5}{20}$
A	$\frac{1}{12}$	R	$\frac{12}{15}$	S	$\frac{3}{5}$
N	$\frac{2}{6}$	O	$\frac{11}{15}$		

Who helped write the Declaration of Independence?

$\underline{T}\underline{}\underline{}\underline{}\underline{}\underline{}\underline{}\underline{}\underline{}\underline{}\underline{}\underline{}\underline{}\underline{}\underline{}$
  1   2   3   4   5   6   7   8   9 10 11 12 13 14 15

Name _____

Starting Points

A **decimal** is a number with one or more numbers to the right of a decimal point. A **decimal point** is a dot placed between the ones place and the tens place of a number, such as 2.5.

Decimals are added and subtracted in the same way as other numbers. Simply carry down the decimal point to your answer.

Directions: Add or subtract.

Examples:

```
   1
  1.3          4.5
 +2.8         -2.2
  4.1          2.3
```

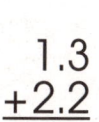

```
  1.3          4.6          5.1          6.7
 +2.2         -3.4         +8.8         -4.3
```

```
  7.9          6.4         11.4          0.5
 -3.7         +8.7         - 9.5         +3.6
```

9.3 + 1.2 = ____   2.5 - 0.7 = ____   1.2 + 5.0 = ____

Bob jogs around the school every day. The distance for one time around is .7 of a mile. If he jogs around the school two times, how many miles does he jog each day? _____

25

Name _____

A Money Message

Directions: What's the smartest thing to do with your money? To find out, solve the following problems and write the matching letter above the answer.

___ ___ ___ ___   ___ ___ ,
$42.71 $33.94 $50.42 $100.73 $45.70 $2.39

___ ___ ___   ___ ___   ___ ___ ___ ___
$33.94 $26.13 $88.02 $45.70 $2.39 $51.12 $45.70 $11.01 $11.01

___ ___ ___   ___ ___ !
$33.94 $88.02 $88.02 $55.76 $42.79

V = $42.13 + 8.29   A = $4.56 + 29.38   N = $4.65 + 21.48   S = $23.46 + 19.25

P = $9.31 + 33.48   L = $6.73 + 4.28   E = $81.49 + 19.24   T = $.42 + 1.94 + .03

U = $50.84 + 4.92   I = $7.49 + 38.21

D = $3.04 + 84.98   W = $1.89 + 49.23

26

Name _____

Counting Change

Directions: Subtract the money using decimals to show how much change a person would receive in each of the following.

Example:
Bill had 3 dollars.
He bought a baseball for $2.83.
How much change did he receive?

$3.00
-$2.83
$ .17

Paid 2 dollars.

Paid 1 dollar.

_____   _____

Paid 5 dollars.

Paid 10 dollars.

_____   _____

Paid 4 dollars.

Paid 7 dollars.

_____   _____

Time Intervals

Directions: Write the time shown on each clock.

Example:

      7:15   7:00

_____   _____   _____

_____   _____   _____

_____   _____   _____

Customary and Metric Measurement: Liquid

Customary measurement is the standard system for measuring. It uses pints, quarts, and gallons to measure liquids.

Metric measurement is a system of measurement based on counting by tens. It uses millileters and liters to measure liquids.

2 cups = 1 pint
2 pints = 1 quart
4 quarts = 1 gallon
1,000 milliliters = 1 liter

1 milliliter   1 cup   1 quart   1 liter   1 gallon

Directions: Choose **pints, quarts,** or **gallons** to measure the following objects.

Directions: Choose **milliliters** or **liters** to measure the following objects.

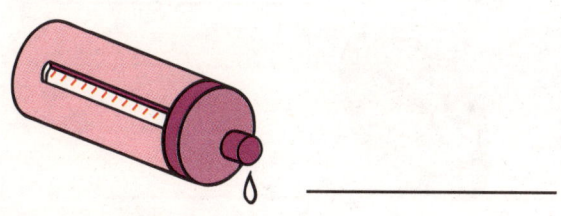

29

Name _____

Customary and Metric Measurement: Weight

Ounces and **pounds** are measurements of weight in the customary measurement system. The ounce is used to measure the weight of very light objects. The pound is used to measure the weight of heavier objects. 16 ounces = 1 pound.

Grams and **kilograms** are measurements of weight in the metric system. A gram weighs about $\frac{1}{28}$ of an ounce. A grape or paper clip weighs about one gram. There are 1,000 grams in a kilogram. A kilogram weighs about 2.2 pounds.

Directions: Choose **ounces** or **pounds** to measure the following objects.

Directions: Choose **grams** or **kilograms** to measure the following objects.

30

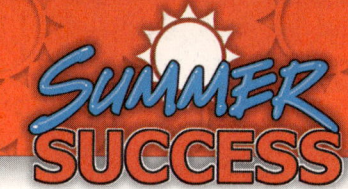

Name _____

Customary and Metric Measurement: Distance

Feet, yards, and **miles** are units of length in the customary system. A foot is equal to 12 inches. A yard is equal to 3 feet. A mile is equal to 1,760 yards.

Directions: Decide whether you would use **foot, yard,** or **mile** to measure each object.

length of a river _____ width of a room _____

height of a tree _____ length of a football field _____

Meters and **kilometers** are units of length in the metric system. A meter is equal to 39.37 inches. A kilometer is equal to about $\frac{5}{8}$ of a mile.

Directions: Decide whether you would use meter or kilometer to measure each object.

height of a door _____ length of a race _____

length of a dress _____ height of a basketball pole _____

1 foot = 12 inches
1 yard = 36 inches or 3 feet
1 mile = 1,760 yards

1 meter = 100 centimeters
1 kilometer = 1,000 meters

Directions: Solve the problems.

Tara races Tom in the 100-meter dash. Tara finishes 10 meters in front of Tom. How many centimeters did Tara finish in front of Tom? _____

Tara races Tom in the 100-yard dash. Tara finishes 10 yards in front of Tom. How many feet did Tara finish in front of Tom? _____

31

Customary and Metric Temperature: Degrees

Fahrenheit is used to measure temperature in the standard system. °F stands for degrees Fahrenheit.

Celsius is used to measure temperature in the metric system. °C stands for degrees Celsius.

Directions: Use the thermometers to answer these questions.

At what temperature does water boil in both °F and °C? _____

At what temperature does water freeze in both °F and °C? _____

What is normal body temperature in both °F and °C? _____

Is it a hot or cold day when the temperature is 30°C? _____

Is it a hot or cold day when the temperature is 12°F? _____

Which temperature best describes a hot summer day?
34°F   72°F   93°F   _____

Which temperature best describes an icy winter day?
0°C   15°C   10°C   _____

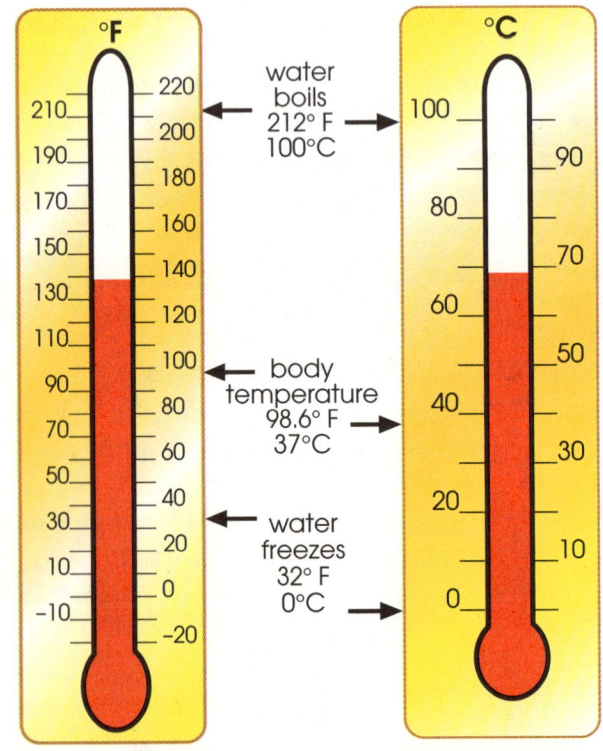

32

Problem Solving...Customary and Metric Style

Directions: Read and solve each problem.

This year, hundreds of people ran in the Capital City Marathon. The race is 4.2 kilometers long. When the first person crossed the finish line, the last person was at the 3.7 kilometer point. How far ahead was the winner?

_____

Dennis crossed the finish line 10 meters ahead of Lucy. Lucy was 5 meters ahead of Sam. How far ahead of Sam was Dennis?

_____

Tony ran 320 yards from school to his home. Then he ran 290 yards to Jay's house. Together Tony and Jay ran 545 yards to the store. How many yards in all did Tony run?

_____

The teacher measured the heights of three children in her class. Marsha was 51 inches tall, Jimmy was 48 inches tall, and Ted was $52\frac{1}{2}$ inches tall. How much taller is Ted than Marsha?_____

How much taller is he than Jimmy?

_____

33

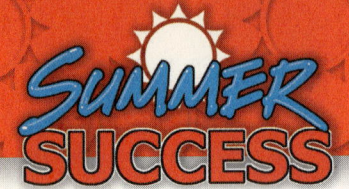

Name _____

Finding Your Way Around

The **perimeter** is the distance around an object. Find the perimeter by adding the lengths of all the sides.

Directions: Find the perimeter for each object (ft. = feet). The first one is done for you.

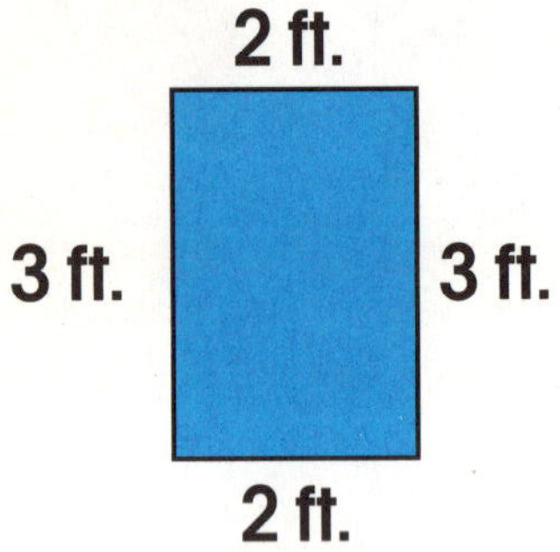

_10 ft._

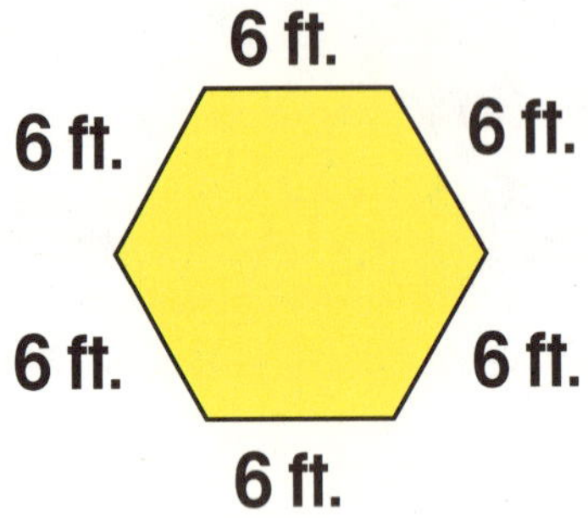

_____   _____

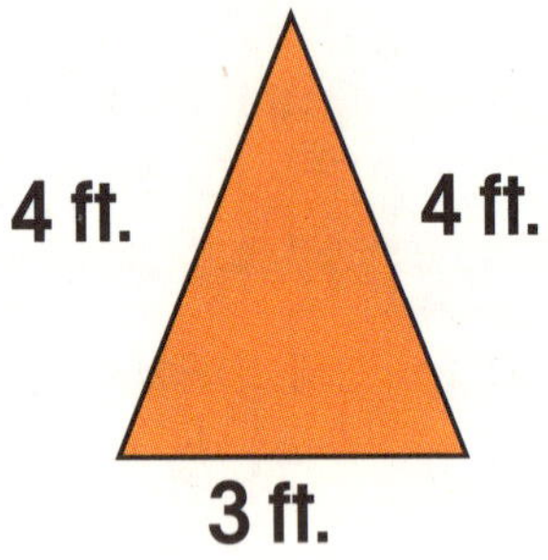

_____   _____   _____

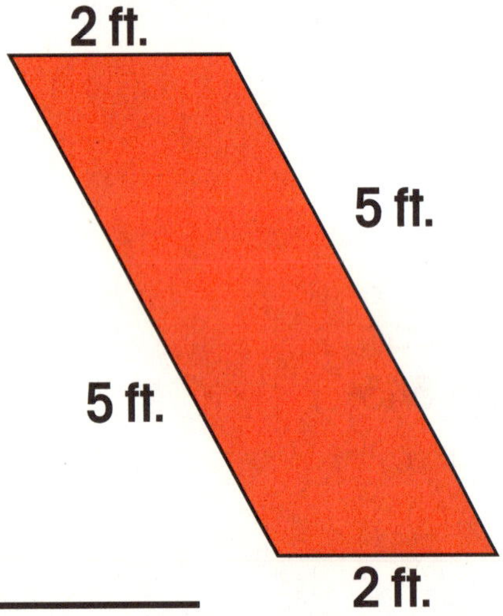

_____   _____   _____

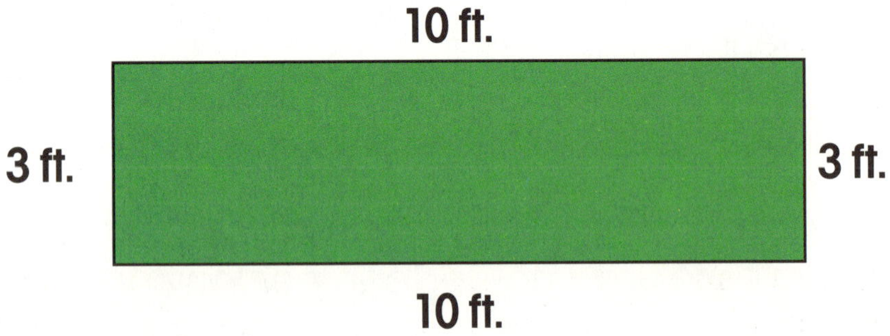

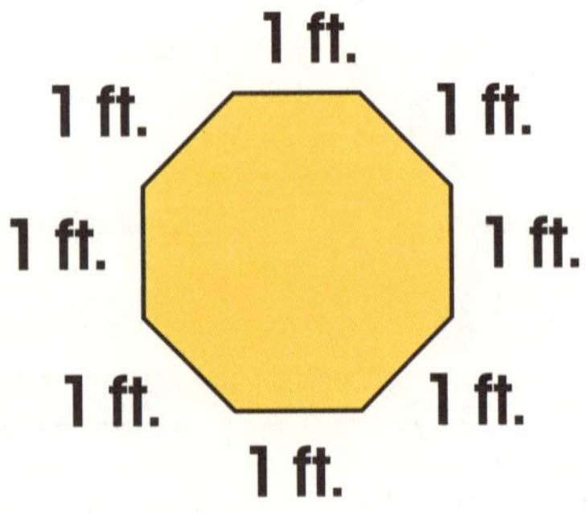

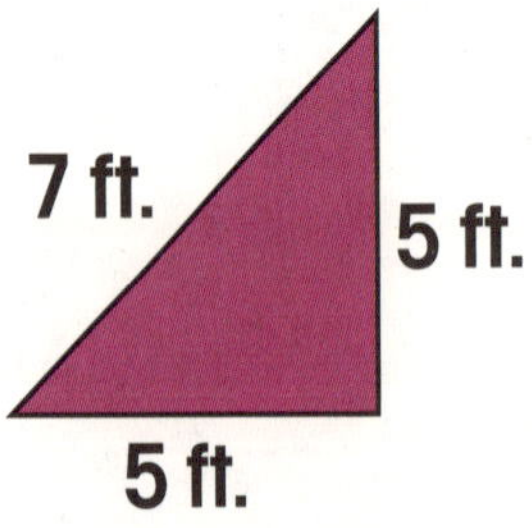

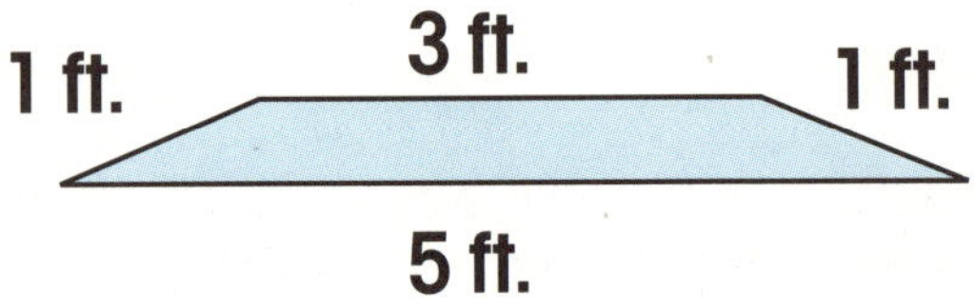

34

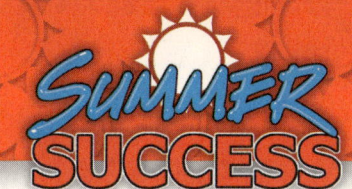

Name _____

Cover the Area

The Local Area Construction Company has been hired by the city to build a recreation center. They will construct a baseball diamond, a basketball court, and a tennis court. How many square feet of land do they need in order to complete each structure? When you want to find the amount of surface in a given boundary, you need to multiply the length by the width. This is called the **area**.

Directions: Find the area of each figure below. (Area = L x W)
Area = square feet

78   Area = _____ sq. ft.

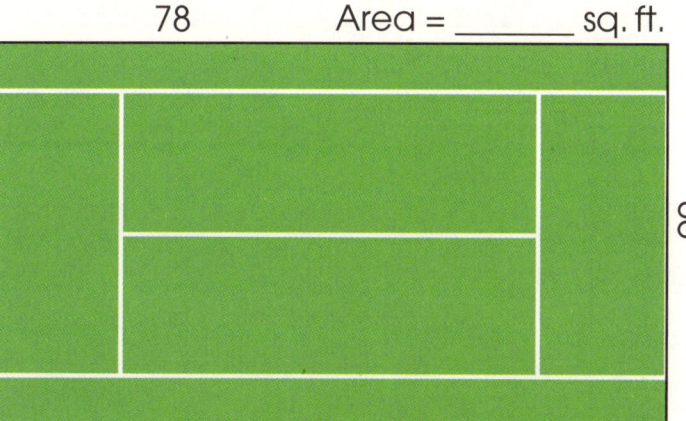

36

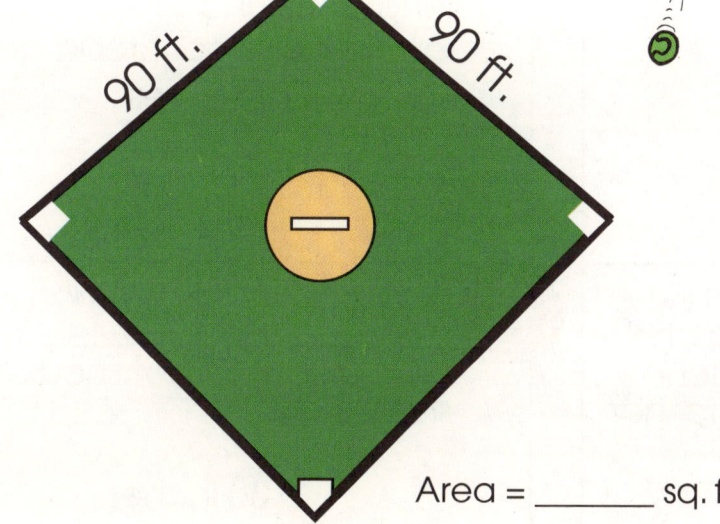

90 ft.   90 ft.

Area = _____ sq. ft.

50 ft.

94 ft.

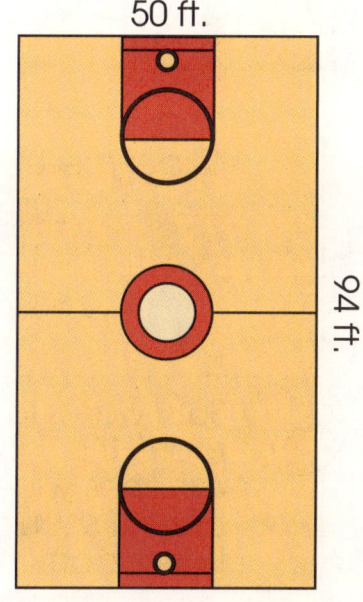

Area = _____ sq. ft.

35

Name _____

Suzy Spider, Interior Decorator

Suzy Spider is decorating her house. She is a very clever decorator, but she needs your help calculating the area and perimeter. Fill in the bubble next to the correct answer.

Area = L x W.
Perimeter = L + W + W + L

1 Suzy is putting a silk fence around her garden. It is 12 inches long and 10 inches wide. What is the perimeter of the garden?
- ○ 22 inches
- ○ 44 inches
- ○ 120 inches

2 Suzy Spider wants to surround her house with a silk thread. Her house is 17 inches long and 12 inches wide. What is its perimeter?
- ○ 29 inches
- ○ 38 inches
- ○ 58 inches

3 Suzy wants to carpet her living room. It is 5 inches long and 4 inches wide. How much carpet should she buy for her living room?
- ○ 9 inches
- ○ 20 inches
- ○ 28 inches

4 Suzy wants to put wallpaper on a kitchen wall. The wall is 7 inches tall and 4 inches wide. What is its area?
- ○ 11 inches
- ○ 28 inches
- ○ 58 inches

5 Suzy has decided to hang a silk thread all the way around her porch. The porch is 4 inches long and 3 inches wide. How long should the thread be?
- ○ 7 inches
- ○ 12 inches
- ○ 14 inches

6 Suzy's bedroom is 6 inches long and 5 inches wide. How much carpet should she buy for it?
- ○ 30 inches
- ○ 60 inches
- ○ 90 inches

Pattern Maze

Directions: Follow the pattern ● ■ ▲ ★ to get through the maze.

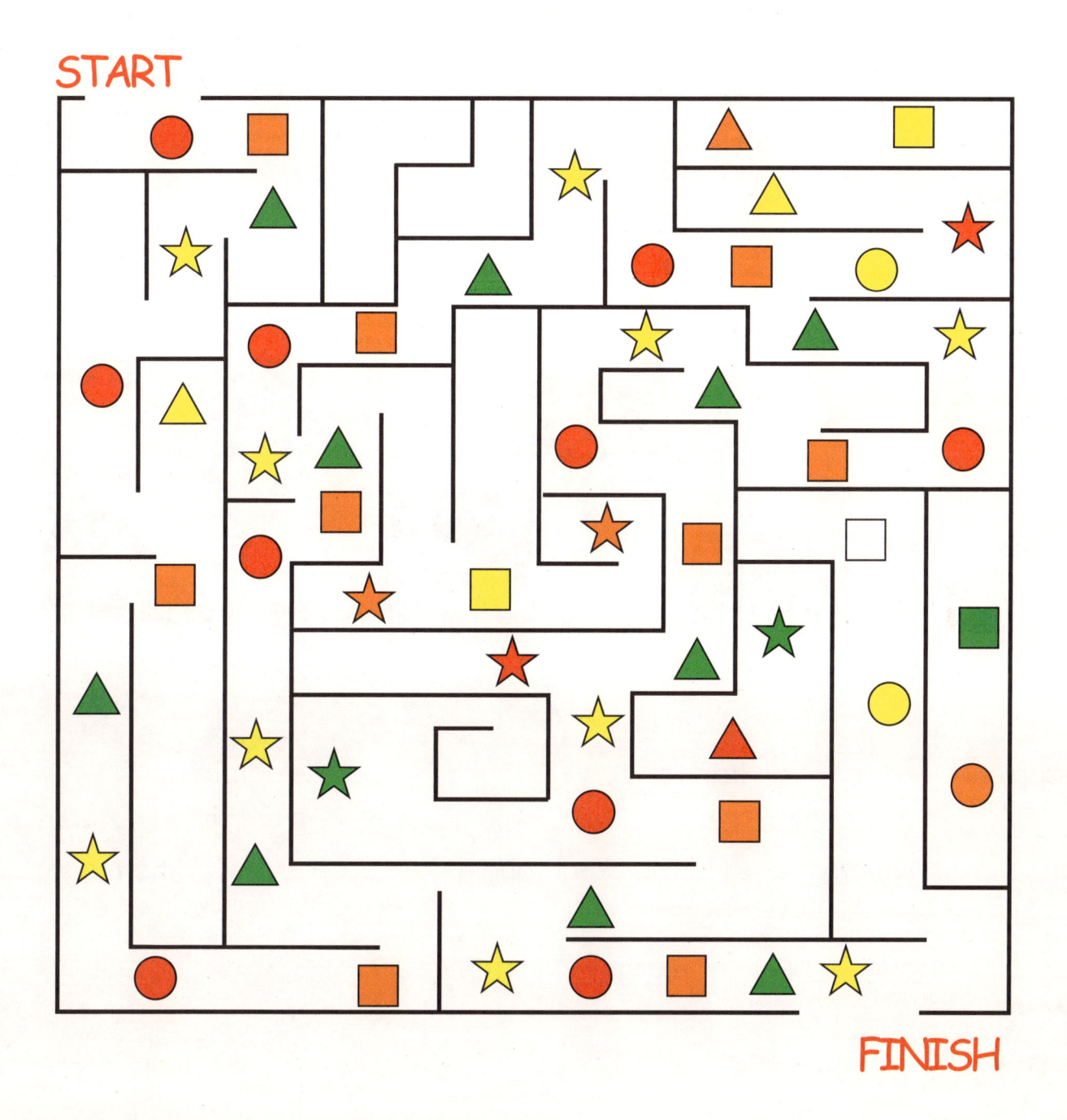

37

Set! Point! Match!

Polygon: A closed figure made with line segments that are joined together.

Triangle: A three-sided polygon.

Square: A figure with four equal sides and four 90 degree angles.

Trapezoid: A polygon with four sides and exactly two sides parallel.

Rectangle: A four-sided polygon with four 90 degree angles.

Parallelogram: A four-sided polygon with opposite sides parallel.

Rhombus: A parallelogram with equal sides.

Directions: Match each polygon to its name.

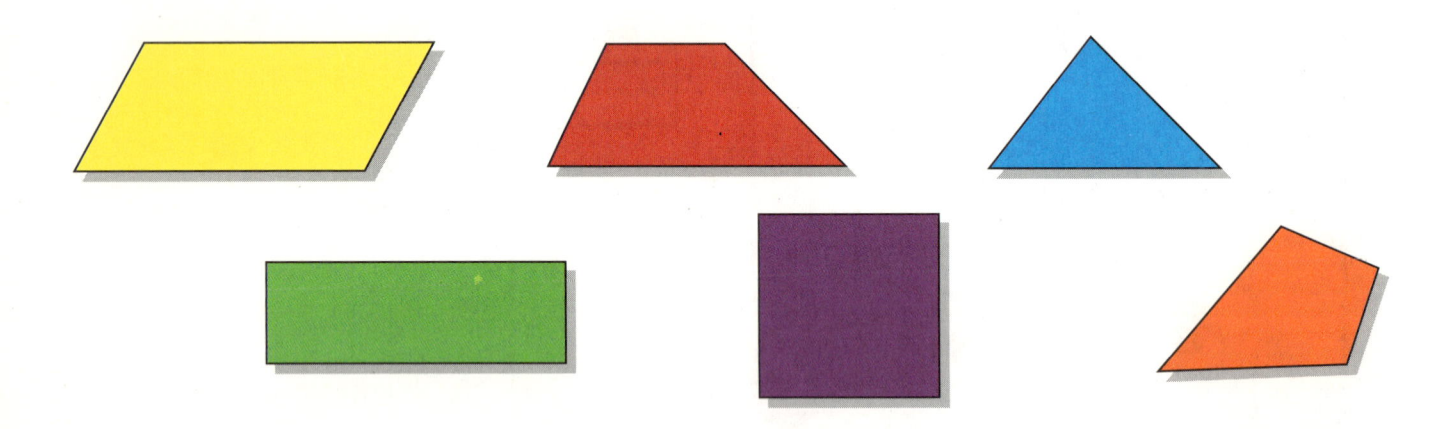

triangle   trapezoid   parallelogram

square   rectangle   rhombus

Name _____

Comparing Polygons

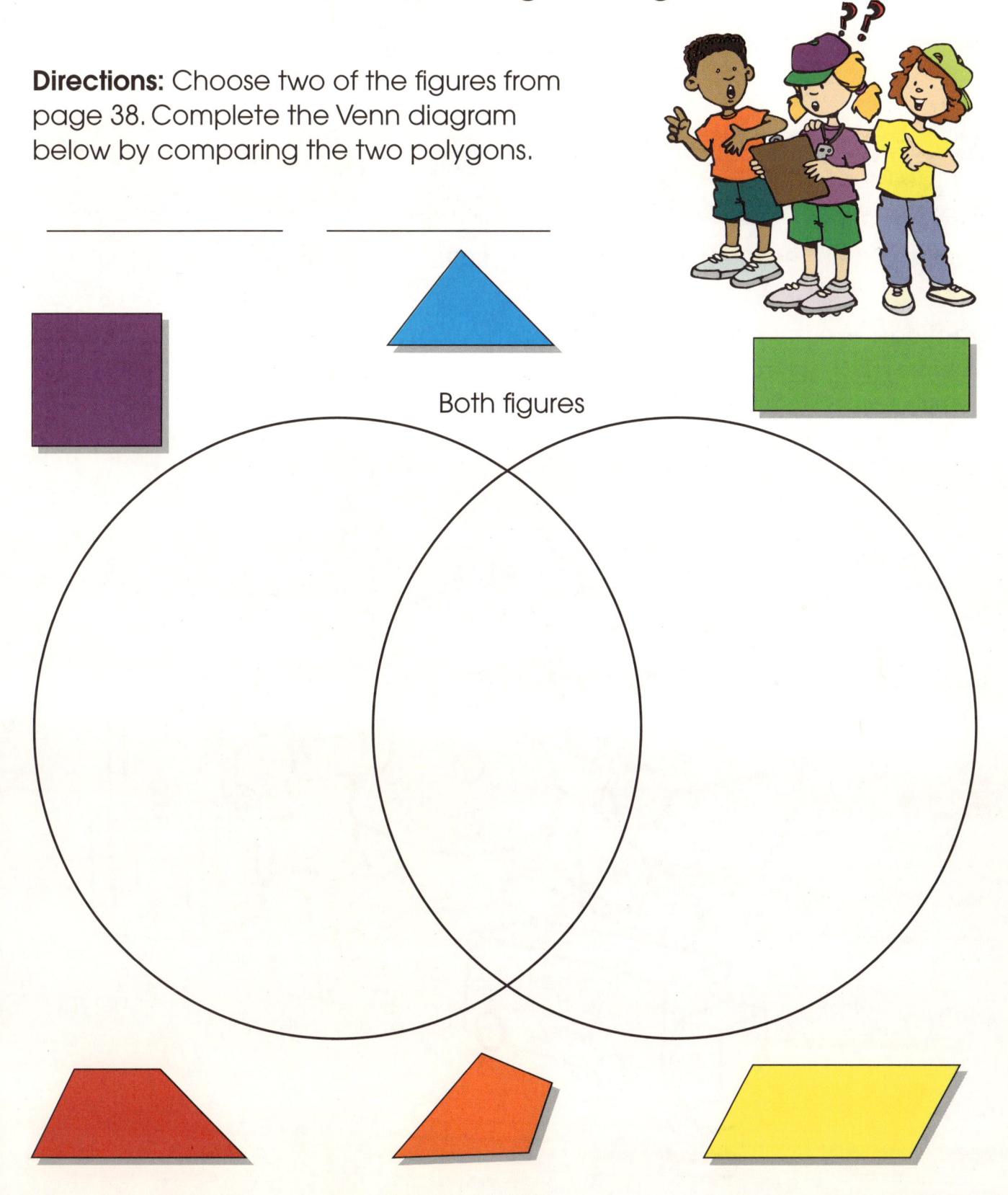

Directions: Choose two of the figures from page 38. Complete the Venn diagram below by comparing the two polygons.

_____   _____

Both figures

39

Geometry

Geometry is the branch of mathematics that has to do with points, lines, and shapes.

cube   rectangular prism   cone   cylinder   sphere

Directions: Use the code to color the picture.

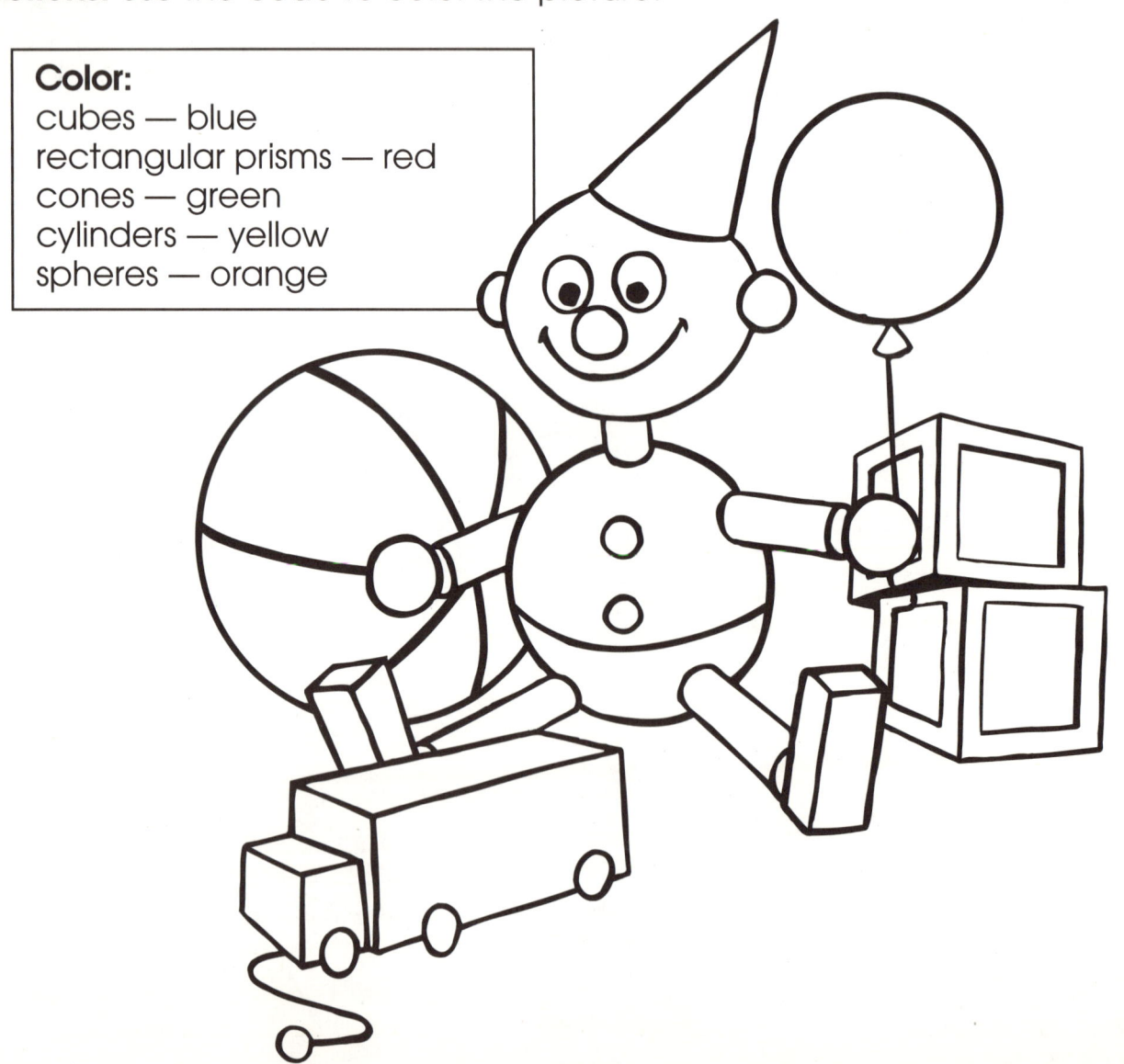

Color:
cubes — blue
rectangular prisms — red
cones — green
cylinders — yellow
spheres — orange

Congruent figures have the same shape and size.
Similar figures have the same shape but different size.
Symmetric figures are those with both sides or parts the same.

Directions: Label each set of figures below either **congruent** or **similar**. Then label if they are **symmetric** or **not symmetric**.

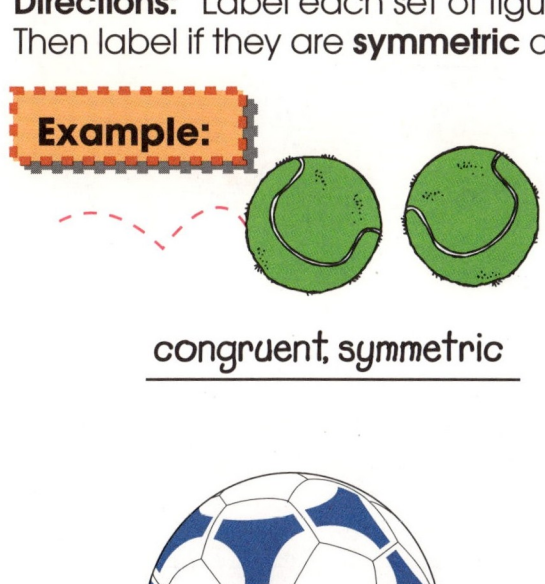

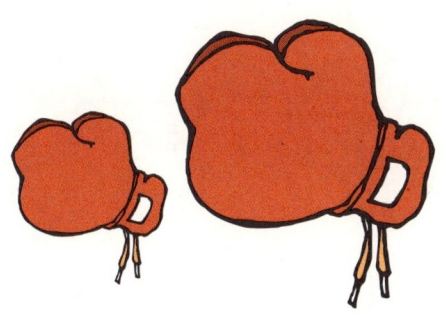

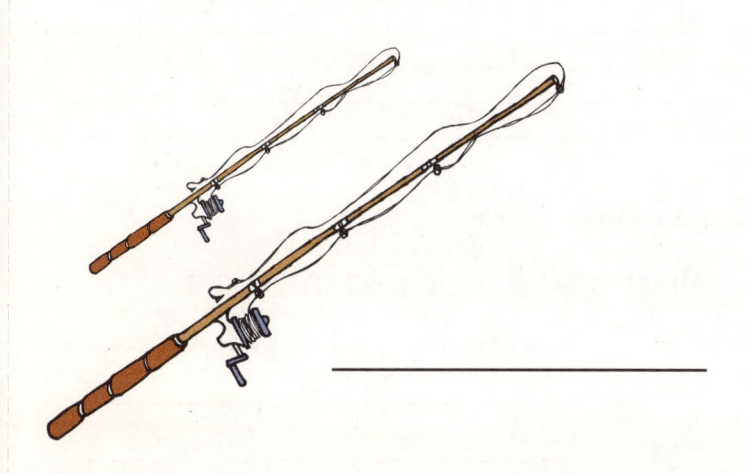

Example:

congruent, symmetric

_____

_____

_____

_____

41

Candy Sales

Every year the students at Lincoln Elementary sell candy as a fund-raising project. These are the results of the sales for this year. They can show their sales on a **bar graph**, which displays information by lengths of parallel rectangular bars.

Grade Level	Number of Sales
Kindergarten	40
First	70
Second	50
Third	80
Fourth	85
Fifth	75

Directions: Color the bar graph to show the number of sales made at each grade level.

Write the grade levels in order starting with the one that sold the most.

1. _____
2. _____
3. _____
4. _____
5. _____
6. _____

Connecting Coordinates

Coordinates are points located on a graph.

Directions: Locate the points on the grid and color in each box.

(across, up)
(4, 7)	(4, 1)	(7, 1)	(3, 5)	(2, 8)	(8, 6)	(4, 8)	(3, 7)
(5, 4)	(6, 5)	(5, 5)	(6, 6)	(7, 3)	(8, 5)	(10, 5)	(4, 3)
(7, 6)	(4, 6)	(1, 8)	(6, 4)	(7, 2)	(4, 5)	(9, 6)	(4, 9)
(3, 6)	(7, 5)	(5, 6)	(4, 2)	(4, 4)	(7, 4)	(2, 7)	(3, 8)

What animal did you form? _____

Probability

One thinking skill to get your brain in gear is figuring probability. **Probability** is the likelihood or chance that something will happen. Probability is expressed and written as a ratio.

The probability of tossing heads or tails on a coin is one in two (1:2).

The probability of rolling any number on a die is one in six (1:6).

The probability of getting a red on this spinner is two in four (2:4).

The probability of drawing an ace from a deck of cards is four in fifty-two (4:52).

Directions: Write the probability ratios to answer these questions.

1. There are 26 letters in the alphabet. What is the probability of drawing any letter from a set of alphabet cards? _____

2. Five of the 26 alphabet letters are vowels. What is the probability of drawing a vowel from the alphabet cards? _____

3. Matt takes 10 shots at the basketball hoop. Six of his shots are baskets. What is the probability of Matt's next shot being a basket? _____

4. A box contains 10 marbles: 2 white, 3 green, 1 red, 2 orange, and 2 blue. What is the probability of pulling a green marble from the box? _____

   A red marble? _____

5. What is the probability of pulling a marble that is not blue? _____

Name _____

Synonyms Riddle

Synonyms are words that mean the same, or almost the same, thing.

Directions: Write a word from the box that is a synonym for each word.

| evening | heat | eat | prepare | guess |
| fuss | wish | relax | explain | glance |

1. worry   __ △ __ __

2. estimate   __ __ __ △ __

3. night   __ __ △ __ __ __ __

4. devour   __ △ __

5. make   __ __ __ △ __ __ __

6. warm   __ △ __ __

7. clarify   __ __ __ __ __ △

8. look   __ __ __ △ __

9. desire   __ △ __ __

10. rest   __ __ △ __ __

Directions: Use the letters in the triangles to answer the riddle.
(**Hint:** Read down.)

Tommy: My pen just fell down the drain. What should I do?

Harold: __ __ __   __   __ __ __ __ __ __ !

45

Opposites Attract

Antonyms are words with opposite meanings.

Directions: Use the words in the box to write the antonym for each word.

same	sadness	light	far
warm	boring	pollute	nothing
shrink	give	conceal	smooth
here	open	dry	sunrise

1. cool — 1. _____
2. dark — 2. _____
3. close — 3. _____
4. everything — 4. _____
5. sunset — 5. _____
6. happiness — 6. _____
7. different — 7. _____
8. show — 8. _____
9. wrinkle — 9. _____
10. moist — 10. _____
11. clean — 11. _____
12. near — 12. _____
13. take — 13. _____
14. interesting — 14. _____
15. expand — 15. _____
16. there — 16. _____

Homophones

Homophones are words with the same pronunciation but different meanings and spellings.

Directions: Circle the correct word to complete each sentence. Then write the word on the line.

1. I am going to _____ a letter to my grandmother.
   right, write

2. Draw a circle around the _____ answer.
   right, write

3. Wait an _____ before going swimming.
   our, hour

4. This is _____ house.
   our, hour

5. He got a _____ from his garden.
   beat, beet

6. Our football team _____ that team.
   beat, beet

7. Go to the store and _____ a loaf of bread.
   by, buy

8. We will drive _____ your house.
   by, buy

9. It will be trouble if the dog _____ the cat.
   seas, sees

10. They sailed the seven _____ .
    seas, sees

11. We have _____ cars in the garage.
    to, too, two

12. I am going _____ the zoo today.
    to, too, two

13. My little brother is going, _____ .
    to, too, two

47

Idioms

Idioms are a colorful way of saying something ordinary. The words in idioms do not mean exactly what they say.

Directions: Read the idioms listed below. Draw a picture of the literal meaning. Then match the idiom to its correct meaning.

	Jump on the bandwagon!	She doesn't eat very much.
	She eats like a bird.	Keep the secret.
	Don't cry over spilled milk!	Make sure you don't miss an opportunity.
	Don't let the cat out of the bag!	Get involved!
	You are the apple of my eye.	Don't worry about things that have already happened.
	Don't miss the boat.	I think you are special.

A New Beginning

A **prefix** is a syllable at the beginning of a word that changes its meaning.

Directions: Add a prefix to the beginning of each word in the box to make a word with the meaning given in each sentence below. The first one is done for you.

PREFIX	MEANING
bi	two or twice
en	to make
in	within
mis	wrong
non	not or without
pre	before
re	again
un	not

grown   write   information   large   cycle   usual   school   sense

1. Jimmy's foot hurt because his toenail was (growing within). __ingrown__

2. If you want to see what is in the background, you will have to (make bigger) the photograph. _____

3. I didn't do a very good job on my homework, so I will have to (write it again) it. _____

4. The newspaper article about the event has some (wrong facts). _____

5. I hope I get a (vehicle with two wheels) for my birthday. _____

6. The story he told was complete (words without meaning)! _____

7. Did you go to (school that comes before kindergarten) before you went to kindergarten? _____

8. The ability to read words upside down is most (not usual). _____

A Means to an End

Suffixes are word parts added to the ends of words. Suffixes change the meaning of words.

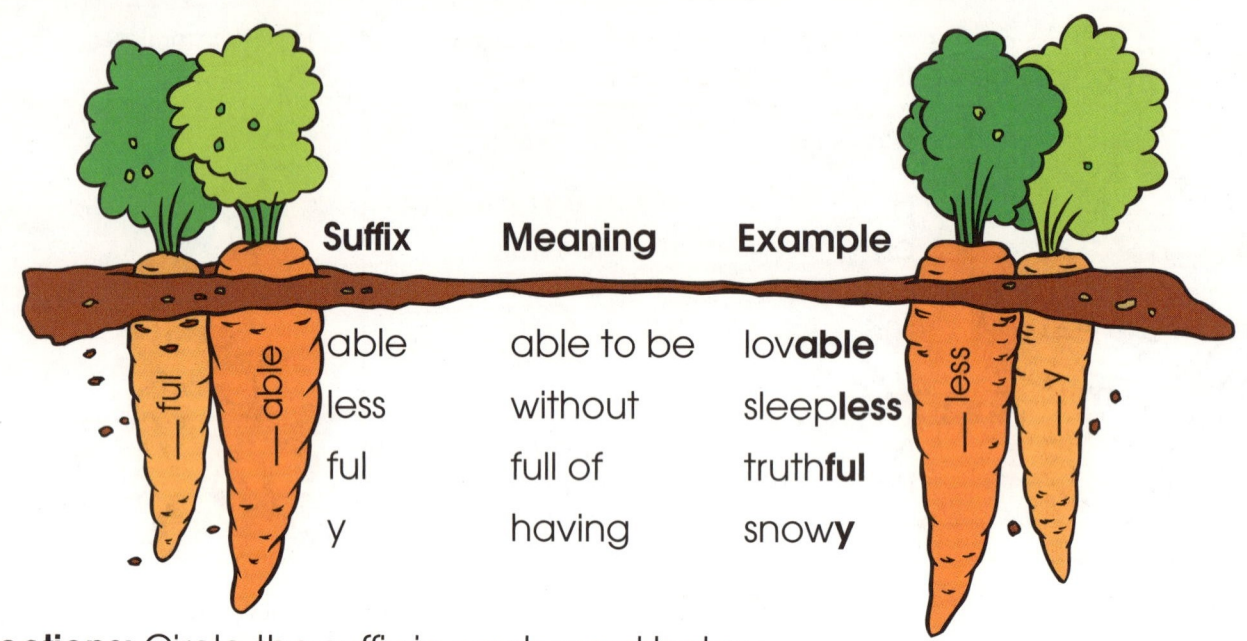

Suffix	Meaning	Example
able	able to be	lov**able**
less	without	sleep**less**
ful	full of	truth**ful**
y	having	snow**y**

Directions: Circle the suffix in each word below.

Example: fluff(y)

rainy   thoughtful   likeable

blameless   enjoyable   helpful

peaceful   careless   silky

Directions: Write a word for each meaning.

full of hope   _____   having rain   _____

without hope   _____   able to break   _____

without power   _____   full of cheer   _____

50

At the Root of It All

A word without any prefixes or suffixes is called a **base word** or **root word**. Prefixes and suffixes change a base word's meaning.

Example: The base word in **defrosted** is **frost**. The prefix is **de** and the suffix is **ed**.

de-frost-ed

Directions: Write the prefix and suffix that was added to each base word.

Prefix	Word	Suffix
1. _____	reconsidered	_____
2. _____	invaluable	_____
3. _____	unstoppable	_____
4. _____	disinterested	_____
5. _____	recoverable	_____
6. _____	inconsiderately	_____
7. _____	misinformed	_____
8. _____	unchanging	_____
9. _____	unlikely	_____
10. _____	distrustful	_____

The Long and Short of It

Directions: Fill in the bubble next to the correct word that has the same vowel sound as the first word in each row.

1. huge	○ bug	○ team	○ bib	○ few
2. seal	○ mice	○ meet	○ whole	○ side
3. lock	○ luck	○ pot	○ cloak	○ load
4. ran	○ rain	○ sit	○ pat	○ race
5. us	○ bun	○ use	○ fuse	○ box
6. ride	○ rain	○ road	○ pie	○ rip
7. sit	○ map	○ find	○ ties	○ fill
8. bone	○ time	○ soap	○ band	○ bond
9. jet	○ jeans	○ bean	○ red	○ jut
10. paid	○ pad	○ main	○ lad	○ lied

Diphthongs

Diphthongs are two vowels together that make a new sound.

Examples:
oi
coin

oy
boy

ew
new

Directions: Fill in the bubble next to the word that has the same vowel sound as the first word in the row.

1.	**join**	○ turmoil	○ fowl	○ few
2.	**toy**	○ loyal	○ lone	○ town
3.	**voice**	○ dove	○ vase	○ annoy
4.	**flew**	○ well	○ newspaper	○ crow
5.	**coil**	○ clean	○ enjoy	○ clue
6.	**decoy**	○ drew	○ dawn	○ royal
7.	**renew**	○ stew	○ coin	○ glow
8.	**loyal**	○ low	○ soil	○ towel
9.	**employ**	○ power	○ join	○ umpire
10.	**moist**	○ jewel	○ just	○ joy
11.	**review**	○ choice	○ avoid	○ chew
12.	**threw**	○ throw	○ view	○ toy
13.	**void**	○ oyster	○ due	○ vendor
14.	**knew**	○ crew	○ know	○ annoy

To Grandmother's House

A **compound** word is formed when two independent words come together.

Example: My father just bought a new **lawnmower**.

Directions: Find the path to Grandmother's house by coloring each stepping stone brown that contains a compound word.

- bread
- father
- refrigerator
- cookbook
- housework
- grandmother
- supermarket
- platter
- grandfather
- visitors
- milk
- turkey
- Thanksgiving
- football
- grandparents
- television
- overstuffed
- potatoes
- vegetables
- dinner
- drumsticks
- bellyache
- applesauce
- driveway

Contractions

Contractions are shortened forms of two words. We use apostrophes to show where letters are missing.

Example: It is = it's

Directions: Write the words that are used in each contraction.

we're _____ + _____   they'll _____ + _____

you'll _____ + _____   aren't _____ + _____

I'm _____ + _____   isn't _____ + _____

Directions: Write the contraction for the two words shown.

you have _____   have not _____

had not _____   we will _____

they are _____   he is _____

she had _____   it will _____

I am _____   is not _____

Capitalization and Commas

We **capitalize** the names of cities and states. We use a **comma** to separate the name of a city and a state.

Directions: Use capital letters and commas to write the names of the cities and states correctly.

Example:
   sioux falls south dakota   <u>Sioux Falls, South Dakota</u>

1. plymouth massachusetts   _____

2. boston massachusetts   _____

3. philadelphia pennsylvania   _____

4. white plains new york   _____

5. newport rhode island   _____

6. yorktown virginia   _____

7. nashville tennessee   _____

8. portland oregon   _____

9. mansfield ohio   _____

Perfectly Punctuated

A statement ends with a period. (.)
A question ends with a question mark. (?)
An exclamation ends with an exclamation mark. (!)

Directions: Write the correct punctuation mark in each box.

1. Every Saturday morning we help a senior citizen ☐
2. Would you like to help us this Saturday ☐
3. You can help me gather the supplies we will need ☐
4. Today we are raking Mrs. Ray's yard ☐
5. That elm tree is huge ☐
6. Will you help them rake the backyard ☐
7. Don't mow too close to the flowers ☐
8. Mrs. Ray has left lemonade there for us ☐
9. I will mow the front yard ☐
10. Will you sweep the front walks ☐
11. She thinks the yard looks super ☐
12. What will we do next Saturday ☐

You Name It!

Nouns are words that tell the names of people, places, or things.

Directions: Write nouns that name people.

1. Could you please give this report to my _____?

2. The _____ works many long hours to plant crops.

3. I had to help my little _____ when he wrecked his bike yesterday.

Directions: Write nouns that name places.

4. I always keep my library books on top of the _____ so I can find them.

5. We enjoyed watching the kites flying high in the _____.

6. Dad built a nice fire in the _____ to keep us warm.

Directions: Write nouns that name things.

7. The little _____ purred softly as I held it.

8. Wouldn't you think a _____ would get tired of carrying its house around all day?

9. The _____ scurried into its hole with the piece of cheese.

10. I can tell by the writing that this _____ is mine.

11. Look at the _____ I made in art.

12. His _____ blew away because of the strong wind.

Tricky Plurals

A **plural** is a form of a word that names or refers to more than one person or thing. Some words have special plural forms.

Example: leaf leaves

Directions: Some of the words in the box are special plurals. Complete each sentence with a plural from the box. Then write the letters from the boxes in the blanks below to solve the puzzle.

tooth	teeth
child	children
foot	feet
mouse	mice
woman	women
man	men

1. I lost my two front ___ ___ ___[ ]___ !

2. My sister has two pet ___ ___ ___[ ]___ .

3. Her favorite book is Little ___ ___ ___[ ]___ .

4. The circus clown had big ___ ___ ___[ ]___ .

5. The teacher played a game with the ___ ___[ ]___ ___ ___ ___ ___ .

Take good care of this pearly plural!

___ ___ ___ ___ ___
 1   2   3   4   5

Pronouns

Pronouns are words that are used in place of nouns.
Examples: he, she, it, they, him, them, her, him

Directions: Read each sentence. Write the pronoun that takes the place of each noun.

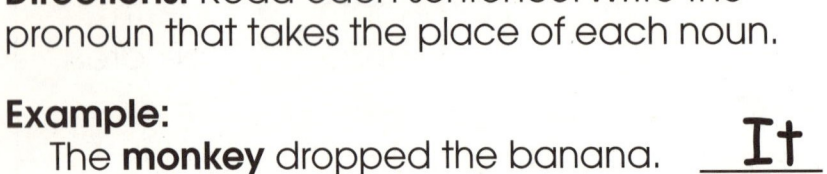

Example:
   The **monkey** dropped the banana.   __It__

1. **Dad** washed the car last night.   _____

2. **Mary and David** took a walk in the park.   _____

3. **Peggy** spent the night at her grandmother's house.   _____

4. The baseball **players** lost their game.   _____

5. **Mike Van Meter** is a great soccer player.   _____

6. The **parrot** can say five different words.   _____

7. **Megan** wrote a story in class today.   _____

8. They gave a party for **Teresa**.   _____

9. Everyone in the class was happy for **Ted**.   _____

10. The children petted the **giraffe**.   _____

11. Linda put the **kittens** near the warm stove.   _____

12. **Gina** made a chocolate cake for my birthday.   _____

13. **Pete and Matt** played baseball on the same team.   _____

14. Give the books to **Herbie**.   _____

Smooth Sailing

A **verb** is a word that can show action. A verb can also tell what someone or something is or is like.

Examples: The boats **sail** on Lake Michigan.
We **eat** dinner at 6:00.
I **am** ten years old.
The clowns **were** funny.

Directions: Circle the verb in each sentence.

1. John sips milk.
2. They throw the football.
3. We hiked in the woods.
4. I enjoy music.
5. My friend smiles often.
6. A lion hunts for food.
7. We ate lunch at noon.
8. Fish swim in the ocean.
9. My team won the game.
10. They were last in line.
11. The wind howled during the night.
12. Kangaroos live in Australia.
13. The plane flew into the clouds.
14. We recorded the song.
15. They forgot the directions.

Verb Tenses

Examples:

  Present Tense She helps him study.

  Past Tense   She helped him study.

  Future Tense She will help him study.

Directions: Write the past tense of these verbs.

  see _____

  walk _____

  sit _____

  change _____

Directions: Write the future tense of these verbs.

  sleep _____

  sing _____

Directions: Change the boldfaced verb to the tense shown in the parenthesis.

1. He **ate** his lunch with two friends. (future tense) _____

2. Paula and her father **will run** two laps. (past tense) _____

3. Mrs. jones **called** her sister in California. (present tense) _____

4. Julie's grandmother **gave** her a new puppy for her birthday. (future tense) _____

5. Andy **will ride** his bicycle after school. (present tense) _____

6. Molly **babysits** for her younger brother and sister on Saturdays. (past tense) _____

Awesome Adjectives

Adjectives tell more about nouns. Adjectives are describing words.

Examples: scary animals   **bright** glow   **wet** frog

Directions: Add at least two adjectives to each sentence below. Use your own words or words from the box.

| pale | soft | sticky | burning | furry | glistening | peaceful |
| faint | shivering | slippery | gleaming | gentle | foggy | tangled |

Example: The stripe was blue.
The wide stripe was light blue.

1. The frog had eyes.
   _____

2. The house was a sight.
   _____

3. A boy heard a noise.
   _____

4. The girl tripped over a toad.
   _____

5. A tiger ran through the room.
   _____

6. They saw a glow in the window.
   _____

7. A pan was sitting on the stove.
   _____

8. The boys were eating French fries.
   _____

Adverbs Away!

Adverbs tell when, where, or how about the verb in a sentence. Many adverbs end in **ly** when answering the question, "How?"

Examples: I celebrated my birthday **today**. (When?)
Children sat **near** me. (Where?)
I **excitedly** opened my gifts. (How?)

Directions: Underline the adverb in each sentence. Then, write **when, where** or **how** on the line to tell which question it answers.

1. The children played quietly at home.
   __how__

2. We went to the movie yesterday.
   _____

3. My friends came inside to play.
   _____

4. The child cut his meat carefully.
   _____

5. The girls ran upstairs to get their coats.
   _____

6. The play-off games start tomorrow.
   _____

7. The boys walked slowly.
   _____

8. The teacher said, "Write your name neatly."
   _____

Classifying

Directions: Read the story. Find words in the story that belong in the lists below. Write the words under the correct lists.

    Meg, Joey, and Ryan are talking about what they want to do when they grow up. Meg says, "I want to be a great writer. I'll write lots of books and articles for newspapers and magazines."
    "I want to be a famous athlete," says Joey. "I'll play baseball in the summer and football in the fall."
    "Oh, yes," adds Meg. "I want to be a famous tennis star, too. When I'm not busy writing books, I'll play in tournaments all over the world. I'll be the world's champion!"
    Ryan says, "That sounds pretty good. But I think I'll be a doctor and a carpenter. I'll build my very own cabin that I can live in during the winter."
    "I'm going to live in a lighthouse by the sea," says Joey. "I've always wanted to do that. Then I can go fishing any time I want."
    "I suppose I'll live in a castle when I grow up," says Meg. "World champion tennis players make lots of money!"

Jobs

1. _____
2. _____
3. _____
4. _____

Sports

1. _____
2. _____
3. _____
4. _____

Seasons

1. _____
2. _____
3. _____

Houses

1. _____
2. _____
3. _____

The Maya Indians

The **main idea** is sometimes stated in one of the sentences of a paragraph. Other sentences in the paragraph give more information about the main idea. These other bits of information are called **supporting details**.

Directions: Read the paragraphs and answer the questions.

Mayan scholars made cultural advances in astronomy and mathematics. They studied the Moon and the planets. They also made accurate records and predictions of their cycles. They developed two calendars. One calendar predicted good or bad luck. The second calendar, like ours, had 365 days. The Mayans had a number system that consisted of dots and bars. The Mayans were probably the first people to use the concept of zero.

1. What is the main idea? _____

2. What are two details that support the main idea? _____

The Mayan heritage continues with many people of Mexico and Central America. More than 20 languages and dialects are said to have developed from the ancient Mayan language. Many of their descendants still carry on some of the traditional religious customs. Also, the ruins of ancient Mayan cities are visited each year by many tourists.

3. What is the main idea? _____

4. What are two details that support the main idea? _____

Benjamin Franklin

Benjamin Franklin was born in Boston, Massachusetts, on January 17, 1706. Even though he only attended school to age 10, he worked hard to improve his mind and character. He taught himself several foreign languages and learned many skills that would later be a great help to him.

Ben Franklin played a very important part in our history. One of his many accomplishments was as a printer. He was a helper (apprentice) to his half-brother, James, and later moved to the city of Philadelphia where he worked in another print shop.

Another skill that he developed was writing. He wrote and published *Poor Richard's Almanac* in December 1732. Franklin was also a diplomat. He served our country in many ways, both in the United States and in Europe. As an inventor he experimented with electricity. Have you heard about the kite and key experiment? Benjamin Franklin was able to prove that lightning has an electrical discharge.

Directions: Answer these questions about Benjamin Franklin.

1. Fill in the bubble next to the main idea.

    ○ Benjamin Franklin was a very important part of our history.

    ○ Benjamin Franklin wrote Poor Richard's Almanac.

    ○ He flew a kite with a key on the string.

2. How old was Ben Franklin when he left school? _____

3. Write three of Ben Franklin's accomplishments.

    1) _____

    2) _____

    3) _____

Crater Lake

When you come to a word you don't know, look for clues to its meaning in the words around it. These nearby words are called **context clues** and can help you figure out a new word.

> **Example:** Mount Mazama, an ancient volcano, collapsed thousands of years ago, leaving a huge bowl, or crater.
>
> **Context Clues:** thousands, years ago
> **Meaning:** very old

Directions: Fill in the bubble next to the correct meaning of the underlined word.

1. Crater Lake, in the Cascade Mountains of southern Oregon, rests in an inactive volcano at an <u>altitude</u> of about 6,200 feet above sea level.

    ○ height   ○ average

2. No streams or rivers <u>supply</u> the lake with water. Precipitation, in the form of snow and rain, has filled the crater.

    ○ fill   ○ save

3. Crater Lake is the deepest lake in the United States. It is 1,932 feet at its greatest <u>depth</u>.

    ○ far   ○ measurement downward

4. Years ago, a mining <u>prospector</u> was looking for minerals and oil. He saw the lake and called it "Deep Blue Lake" because of its beautiful color.

    ○ explorer   ○ beautiful

5. Crater Lake and the area around it are now part of a National Park. The Park Service will <u>ensure</u> people do not pollute the lake.

    ○ protect   ○ make certain

6. There were no fish in Crater Lake until it was <u>stocked</u> with trout in 1888. People who fish are happy that more fish are still added each year.

    ○ stored   ○ filled

How Plants Get Food

Every living thing needs food. Did you ever wonder how plants get food? They do not sit down and eat a bowl of soup! Plants get their food from the soil and from water. To see how, cut off some stalks of celery. Put the stalks in a clear glass. Fill the glass half full of water. Add a few drops of red food coloring to the water. Leave it overnight. The next day you will see that parts of the celery have turned red! The red lines show how the celery "sucked up" water.

Directions: Answer these questions about how plants get food.

1. Name two ways plants get food.

    1) _____

    2) _____

2. Complete the four steps for using celery to see how plants get food.

    1) Cut off some stalks of _____ .

    2) Put the stalks in _____ .

    3) Fill the glass _____ .

    4) Add a few drops of _____ .

3. What do the red lines in the celery show?

    _____

    _____

Thinking About Spiders

A **fact** is something known to be true or real. An **opinion** is a belief based on what a person thinks rather than what is known to be true.

Directions: Write **F** if the statement is a fact and **O** if it is an opinion.

> Spiders spin webs to build homes that they use as traps to catch insects. By pushing sticky thread out through the backs of their bodies, spiders create the web's design.
>
> Different types of spiders spin different types of webs. Some webs are flat while others are bowl-shaped.
>
> Once an insect is caught in a web, the spider wraps it in silk, kills it, and then unwraps it and sucks out its juices. The torn web is eaten, and a new web is spun.

1. _____ All spiders spin beautiful webs.

2. _____ Spiders are ugly.

3. _____ Bowl-like webs are better than flat webs.

4. _____ Webs are used to trap insects.

5. _____ A spider's prey is wrapped in silk.

6. _____ Spiders eat too much.

7. _____ Spiders eat their own webs.

8. _____ Spiders suck the juices out of their prey.

9. _____ A spider's web is sticky.

10. _____ Everyone is afraid of spiders.

Compare and Contrast

Directions: Look for similarities and differences in the following paragraphs. Then answer the questions.

Phong and Chris both live in the city. They live in the same apartment building and go to the same school. Phong and Chris sometimes walk to school together. If it is raining or storming, Phong's dad drives them to school on his way to work. In the summer, they spend a lot of time at the park across the street from their building.

Phong lives in Apartment 12-A with his little sister and mom and dad. He has a collection of model race cars that he put together with his dad's help. He even has a bookshelf full of books about race cars and race car drivers.

Chris has a big family. He has two older brothers and one older sister. When Chris has time to do anything he wants, he gets out his butterfly collection. He notes the place he found each specimen and the day he found it. He also likes to play with puzzles.

1. Compare Phong and Chris. List at least three similarities.

   _____
   _____
   _____

2. Contrast Phong and Chris. List two differences.

   _____
   _____
   _____

Drawing Conclusions

Drawing a conclusion means to use clues to make a final decision about something. To draw a conclusion, you must read carefully.

Directions: Read each story carefully. Use the clues given to draw a conclusion about the story.

    The boy and girl took turns pushing the shopping cart. They went up and down the aisles. Each time they stopped the cart, they would look at things on the shelf and decide what they needed. Jody asked her older brother, "Will I need a box of 48 crayons in Mrs. Charles' class?"
    "Yes, I think so," he answered. Then he turned to their mother and said, "I need some new notebooks. Can I get some?"

1. Where are they? _____

2. What are they doing there? _____

3. How do you know? Write at least two clue words that helped you.

_____

    Eric and Randy held on tight. They looked around them and saw that they were not the only ones holding on. The car moved slowly upward. As they turned and looked over the side, they noticed that the people far below them seemed to be getting smaller and smaller. "Hey, Eric, did I tell you this is my first time on one of these?" asked Randy. As they started down the hill at a frightening speed, Randy screamed, "And it may be my last!"

1. Where are they? _____

2. How do you know? Write at least two clue words that helped you.

_____

Name _____

Cause and Effect

Cause and effect sentences often use clue words to show the relationship between two events. Common clue words are *because, so, when,* and *since*.

Directions: Read the sentences and circle each clue word. The first one has been done for you.

1. I'll help you clean your room, (so) we can go out to play sooner.

2. Because of the heavy snowfall, school was closed today.

3. She was not smiling, so her mother wanted her school pictures taken again.

4. Mrs. Wilderman came to school with crutches today, because she had a skating accident.

5. When the team began making too many mistakes at practice, the coach told them to take a break.

Name _____

Which Way Down?

Thinking about what might happen next is called **predicting outcomes.**

Directions: Read the story. Then, write a word from the box to complete each sentence.

   Maria and her family enjoy going to Water Slide Park on Saturdays because there are so many fun things to do. Maria's older brother and sister like to go down Daredevil Slide. Maria usually goes down Lazy Falls Slide because it isn't as steep.
   One Saturday, Maria's sister and brother talk her into climbing up Daredevil Slide. They tell her how much fun it is. The lifeguard assures Maria it's safe and promises to watch her. Maria looks down at Daredevil Slide. Then, she looks over at Lazy Falls Slide. Maria feels very brave.

| fun | brave |
| safe | Lazy Falls |

1. Maria usually goes down _____ Slide.

2. Her brother and sister say Daredevil Slide is _____.

3. The lifeguard assures Maria the slide is _____.

4. Looking down Daredevil Slide, Maria feels _____.

Directions: Write a complete sentence to answer each question.

5. What will Maria probably do now? _____

6. What will Maria probably want to do next? _____

74

Name _____

What Are You Reading?

A **fiction** book is a book about things that are made up or not true. Fantasy books are fiction. A **nonfiction** book is about things that have really happened. Books can be classified into more types:

Mystery - books that have clues that lead to solving a problem or mystery

Biography - book about a real person's life

Poetry - a collection of poems, which may or may not rhyme

Fantasy - books about things that cannot really happen

Sports - books about different sports or sport figures

Travel - books about going to other places

Directions: Write *mystery, biography, poetry, fantasy, sports,* or *travel* next to each title.

The Life of Helen Keller _____

Let's Go to Mexico! _____

The Case of the Missing Doll _____

How to Play Golf _____

Turtle Soup and Other Poems _____

Fred's Flying Saucer _____

Name _____

Story Elements

A good story will contain these **story elements:**

Title — gives a clue to what the story is about
Setting — tells where and when the story takes place
Characters — describes people in the story
Plot — explains the events in a story that create a problem
Climax — describes the most thrilling part of the story where the problem will either be solved, or it won't
Resolution — tells how the characters solve the story problem
Conclusion — tells what happens to the characters in the end

Directions: Write the letter of the definition that matches the story element.

1. _____ Setting
2. _____ Characters
3. _____ Plot
4. _____ Climax
5. _____ Resolution
6. _____ Conclusion

a. the way a story ends
b. the changing point of a story; it is often the most exciting part of the story.
c. the series of events in a story involving a problem
d. the place and time
e. people or animals in the story
f. the way in which the problems are solved

Story Webs

A **story web** is a way to visually classify a story.

All short stories have a plot, characters, setting, and a theme.

The **plot** is what the story is about.

The **characters** are the people or animals in the story.

The **setting** is where and when the story occurs.

The **theme** is the message or idea of the story.

Directions: Use the story "Snow White" to complete this story web.

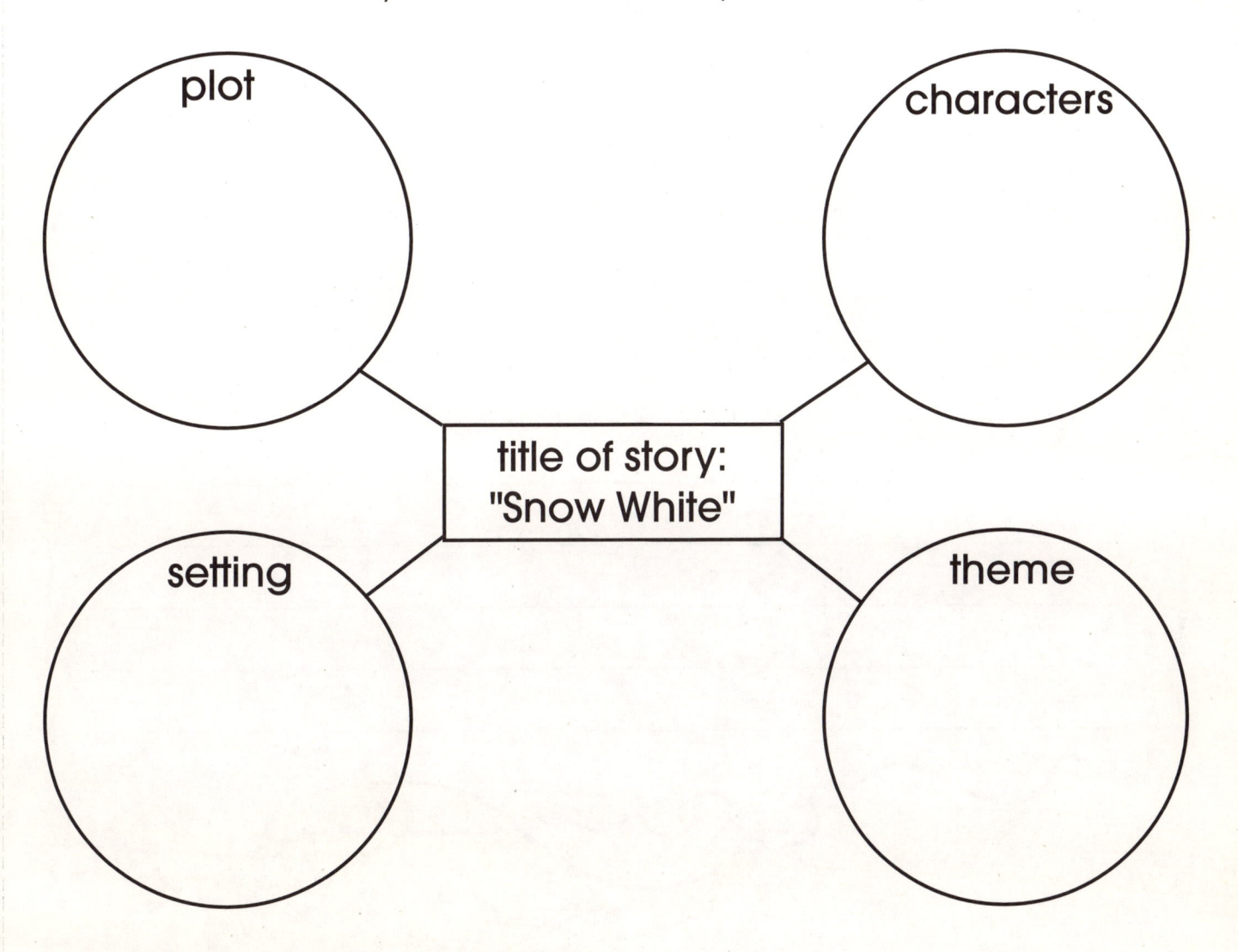

- plot
- characters
- title of story: "Snow White"
- setting
- theme

Name _____

A Series of Wishes

Directions: Read all the sentences. Write the numbers 1—8 in the circles to put the sentences in order. Then, rewrite the sentences in the correct order at the bottom.

○ The traveler began to rub the sand off the lantern.

○ Second, he wished that he could find his family again.

○ The genie said that he would grant the traveler three wishes.

○ A traveler had lost his way as he crossed the desert.

○ His third wish was that he could have three more wishes.

○ As he rubbed the lantern, a genie appeared in a cloud of smoke.

○ The lost traveler found an old lantern lying in the sand.

○ First, the traveler wished that he would find his way out of the desert.

1. _____
2. _____
3. _____
4. _____
5. _____
6. _____
7. _____
8. _____

Name _____

Organize Your Thoughts

An **autobiography** is a written account of your life. An outline can help you to organize details about your life.

Directions: Fill in the outline with information about your life.

I. My Early Years

    A. Birthdate _____ Place _____

    B. Favorite activities _____

    C. Family members _____

    D. Things I learned _____

    E. First school _____

II. My Present

    A. School grade _____

    B. Friends _____

    C. Favorite subjects _____

    D. Sports or hobbies _____

    E. Family fun _____

III. My Future

    A. Middle School/High School _____

    B. College _____

    C. Ambitions _____

    D. Places I would like to see _____

    E. Things I would like to accomplish _____

_____

_____

Name _____

Write Your Own Story

You may want to create a story just for fun! Once you have chosen the kind of story you want to write, you should brainstorm for ideas. But remember, a good story should have a beginning, a middle, and an end. You can use an outline to organize your ideas.

Directions: Write your ideas for a story to complete this outline.

Kind of Story (mystery, adventure, etc.) _____

  I. Setting (where and when the story takes place)

    A. Where _____ Description _____

    _____

    B. When _____

 II. Characters (people in the story)

    A. Name _____ Description _____

    B. Name _____ Description _____

    C. Name _____ Description _____

    D. Name _____ Description _____

III. Plot (events of the story) List main events in order.

    A. _____

    _____

    B. _____

    _____

    C. _____

    _____

    D. _____

    _____

Dictionary Mystery

Directions: Below are six dictionary entries with pronunciations and definitions. The only things missing are the entry words. Write the correct entry words. Be sure to spell each word correctly.

Entry word:

_____

(rōz)
A flower that grows on bushes and vines.

Entry word:

_____

(ra bət)
A small animal that has long ears.

Entry word:

_____

(fäks)
A wild animal that lives in the woods.

Entry word:

_____

(pē än ō)
A musical instrument that has many keys.

Entry word:

_____

(lāk)
A body of water that is surrounded by land.

Entry word:

_____

(bās bȯl)
A game played with a bat and a ball.

Directions: Now write the entry words in alphabetical order.

1. _____
2. _____
3. _____
4. _____
5. _____
6. _____

Right in Between

Guide words tell you the first and last word that appears on a dictionary page. The entry word you are looking for will appear on a page if it comes between the guide words in alphabetical order.

Directions: Underline the words in each group that would be found on a page with the given guide words.

fish / five	evergreen / eye	level / love	pickle / plaster
fight	event	lullaby	pint
fist	edge	leave	polo
first	ewe	look	prize
finish	evil	light	please
file	eagle	loud	planet
frisky	evolve	low	piglet
fit	evaporate	letter	palace

tan / time	heaven / hundred	candle / create	zenith / zone
truck	hairy	coil	zoo
tail	horrible	crater	zinnia
toast	hungry	corner	zodiac
thicket	honest	creep	zest
tepee	hindsight	cavern	zeal
tasty	hunter	candid	zebra
tease	help	cable	zephyr

Alphabetical Order

The words in these lists begin with the same letter.

Directions: Use the second or third letters of each word to put the lists in alphabetical order.

Example:

tiger	_3_ tiger
tape	_1_ tape
tide	_2_ tide

All three words begin with the same letter (**t**), so look at the second letters. The letter **a** comes before **i**, so **tape** comes first. Then look at the third letters in **tiger** and **tide** to see which word comes next.

___ glad

___ goat

___ gasoline

___ gentle

___ grumble

___ answer

___ about

___ ask

___ around

___ against

___ tape

___ taste

___ table

___ talent

___ taught

Glossary of Math, Reading, and Language Arts Terms

addition: the operation that combines numbers to create a sum.

adjective: a describing word that tells more about a noun.

adverb: tells when, where, or how about the verb of a sentence.

antonym: words with opposite, or nearly opposite, meanings.

area: the amount of surface in a given boundary, found by multiplying length by width.

articles: any one of the words *a*, *an*, or *the* used to modify a noun.

autobiography: a written account of your life.

bar graph: displays information by lengths of parallel rectangular bars.

base word (also called root word): the word left after you take off a prefix or a suffix.

Celsius: used to measure temperature in the metric system.

character: a person, animal, or object that a story is about.

climax: the most thrilling part of the story where the problem will or will not be solved.

commutative: a property that allows you to add or multiply two numbers in any order and still get the same answer, such as 2x3=3x2.

conclusion: a final decision about something, or the part of a story that tells what happens to the characters.

congruent: figures that are the same shape and the same size.

contraction: shortened forms of two words often using an apostrophe to show where letters are missing.

coordinates: points located on the same graph.

customary measurement: the standard system for measuring, such as cup, pint, quart, gallon, ounce, pound, inch, foot, yard, mile.

decimal: a number with one or more numbers to the right of a decimal point.

decimal point: a dot placed between the ones place and the tenths place of a number.

denominator: the bottom number in a fraction telling the number of parts in the whole.

difference: the number received when one number is subtracted from another.

digit: a numeral.

diphthongs: two vowels together that make a new sound.

dividend: a number that is to be divided by another number.

division: shows how many times one number contains another.

divisor: a number by which another number is to be divided.

fact: something known to be true.

Fahrenheit: used to measure temperature in the standard system.

fiction: stories that are made up.

fraction: a number that stands for part of a whole.

geometry: the branch of mathematics that has to do with points, lines, and shapes.

homophone: a word with the same pronunciation as another, but with a different meaning, and often a different spelling, such as *son–sun*.

idiom: a figure of speech or phrase that means something different than what the words actually say, such as "He changed his bad habits and *turned over a new leaf.*"

mass: the amount or quantity of matter contained in an object.

metric measurement: a system of measurement based on counting by tens, such as liter, milliliter, gram, kilogram, centimeter, meter, kilometer.

multiplication: taking a number and adding to itself a certain number of times.

nonfiction: stories that are true.

noun: a word that names a person, place, or thing.

numerator: the top number in a fraction showing the number of parts out of the whole.

operations: addition, subtraction, multiplication, division.

opinion: a belief based on what a person thinks instead of what is known to be true.

ordered pair: lists the horizontal and the vertical location of the point, such as (3,4).

perimeter: the distance around an object found by adding the lengths and widths.

place value: shown by where the numeral is in the number.

plot: explains the events in a story that create a problem.

plural: a form of a word that names or refers to more than one person or thing.

polygon: a closed figure that has three or more sides.

prefix: a part that is added to the beginning of a word that changes the word's meaning.

probability: the likelihood or chance that something will happen.

product: the number received when two numbers are multiplied together.

pronoun: a word that is used in place of a noun.

punctuation: the marks that qualify sentences, such as a period, comma, question mark, exclamation point, and apostrophe.

quotient: the number received when a number is divided.

reading strategies: main idea, supporting details, context clues, fact/opinion.

regrouping: borrowing numbers from another column to complete the operation.

remainder: the number left over when a number cannot be divided evenly.

resolution: tells how the characters solve the story problem.

rounding: expressing a number to the nearest ten, hundred, thousand, and so on.

setting: the place and time that a story happens.

subtraction: "taking away" one number from another to find the difference.

suffix: a part added to the end of a word to change the word's meaning.

sum: the number received when two numbers are added together.

symmetry: when both sides of an object are exactly the same.

synonym: words that mean the same, or almost the same, thing.

theme: a message or central idea of the story.

verb: a word that can show action.

verb tense: tells whether the action is happening in the past, present, or future.

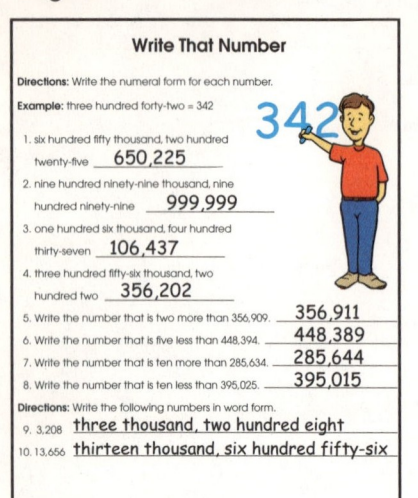

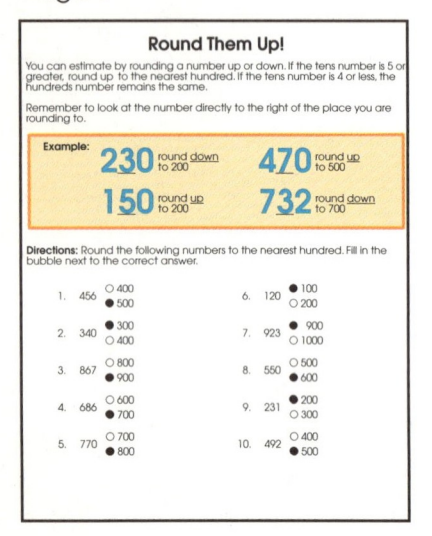

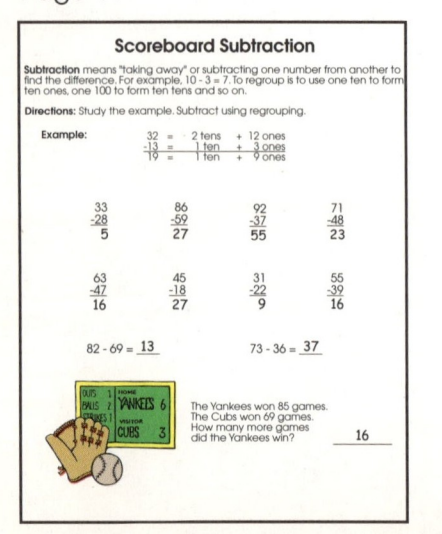

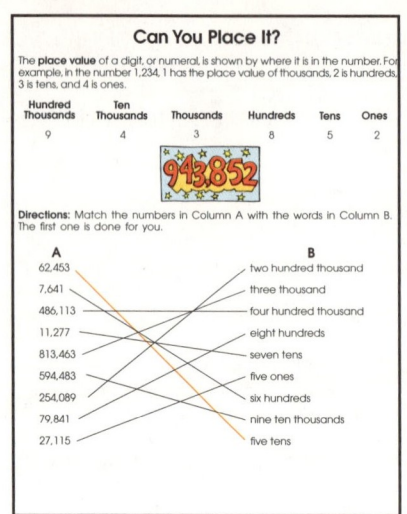

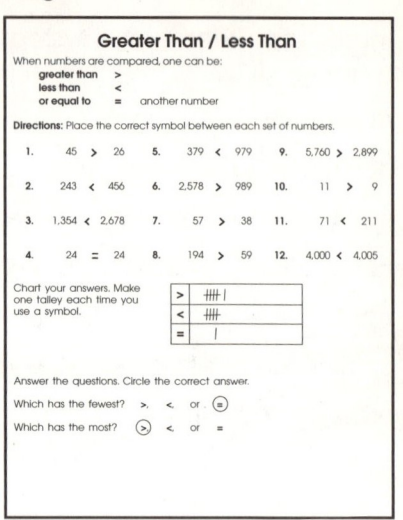

Page 5
Write That Number
Directions: Write the numeral form for each number.

Example: three hundred forty-two = 342

1. six hundred fifty thousand, two hundred twenty-five **650,225**
2. nine hundred ninety-nine thousand, nine hundred ninety-nine **999,999**
3. one hundred six thousand, four hundred thirty-seven **106,437**
4. three hundred fifty-six thousand, two hundred two **356,202**
5. Write the number that is two more than 356,909. **356,911**
6. Write the number that is five less than 448,394. **448,389**
7. Write the number that is ten more than 285,634. **285,644**
8. Write the number that is ten less than 395,025. **395,015**

Directions: Write the following numbers in word form.

9. 3,208 **three thousand, two hundred eight**
10. 13,656 **thirteen thousand, six hundred fifty-six**

Page 6
Can You Place It?
The **place value** of a digit, or numeral, is shown by where it is in the number. For example, in the number 1,234, 1 has the place value of thousands, 2 is hundreds, 3 is tens, and 4 is ones.

Hundred Thousands	Ten Thousands	Thousands	Hundreds	Tens	Ones
9	4	3	8	5	2

943,852

Directions: Match the numbers in Column A with the words in Column B. The first one is done for you.

A	B
62,453	two hundred thousand
7,641	three thousand
486,113	four hundred thousand
11,277	eight hundreds
813,463	seven tens
594,483	five ones
254,089	six hundreds
79,841	nine ten thousands
27,115	five tens

Page 7
Greater Than / Less Than
When numbers are compared, one can be:
- greater than >
- less than <
- or equal to = another number

Directions: Place the correct symbol between each set of numbers.

1. 45 **>** 26
2. 243 **<** 456
3. 1,354 **<** 2,678
4. 24 **=** 24
5. 379 **<** 979
6. 2,578 **>** 989
7. 57 **>** 38
8. 194 **>** 59
9. 5,760 **>** 2,899
10. 11 **>** 9
11. 71 **<** 211
12. 4,000 **<** 4,005

Chart your answers. Make one tally each time you use a symbol.

>	‖‖‖ I
<	‖‖‖
=	I

Answer the questions. Circle the correct answer.

Which has the fewest? >, <, or **=**
Which has the most? **>**, <, or =

Page 8
Round Them Up!
You can estimate by rounding a number up or down. If the tens number is 5 or greater, round up to the nearest hundred. If the tens number is 4 or less, the hundreds number remains the same.

Remember to look at the number directly to the right of the place you are rounding to.

Example:
- 230 round down to 200
- 470 round up to 500
- 1**5**0 round up to 200
- 732 round down to 700

Directions: Round the following numbers to the nearest hundred. Fill in the bubble next to the correct answer.

1. 456 — ● 500 / ○ 400
2. 340 — ● 300 / ○ 400
3. 867 — ○ 800 / ● 900
4. 686 — ● 700 / ○ 600
5. 770 — ● 800 / ○ 700
6. 120 — ● 100 / ○ 200
7. 923 — ● 900 / ○ 1000
8. 550 — ○ 500 / ● 600
9. 231 — ● 200 / ○ 300
10. 492 — ● 500 / ○ 400

Page 9
Leafy Addition
Directions: Add, then color according to the code.

Code:
- green — 79
- orange — 35
- red — 78
- yellow — 87
- purple — 56
- brown — 94

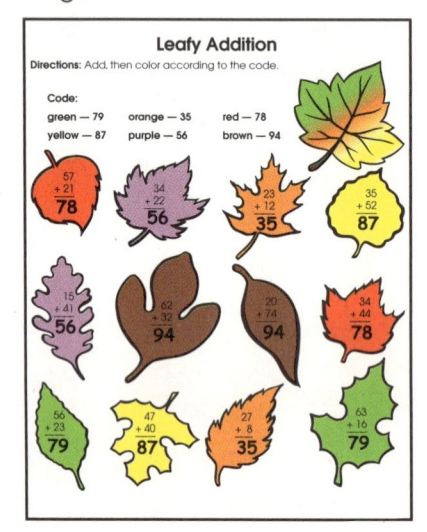

- 67 + 21 = **78**
- 34 + 22 = **56**
- 23 + 12 = **35**
- 35 + 52 = **87**
- 15 + 41 = **56**
- 62 + 32 = **94**
- 20 + 74 = **94**
- 34 + 44 = **78**
- 56 + 23 = **79**
- 47 + 40 = **87**
- 27 + 8 = **35**
- 63 + 16 = **79**

Page 10
Adding-It-Up Puzzle
Sometimes numbers have to be carried to the next column to complete an operation. This is called **regrouping**.

Add the ones. Regroup.	Add the tens. Regroup.	Add the hundreds. Regroup.	Add the thousands. Regroup.
7,465 +4,978 **3**	7,465 +4,978 **43**	7,465 +4,978 **443**	7,465 +4,978 **12,443**

Directions: Add using regrouping. Then use the code to discover the name of a United States president.

- 348 + 752 = 1,100
- 642 + 277 = 919
- 386 + 787 = 1,173
- 184 + 875 = 1,059
- 578 + 874 = 1,452
- 653 + 768 = 1,421
- 653 + 359 = 1,012
- 946 + 239 = 1,185
- 393 + 257 = 650
- 199 + 843 = 1,042
- 721 + 679 = 1,400

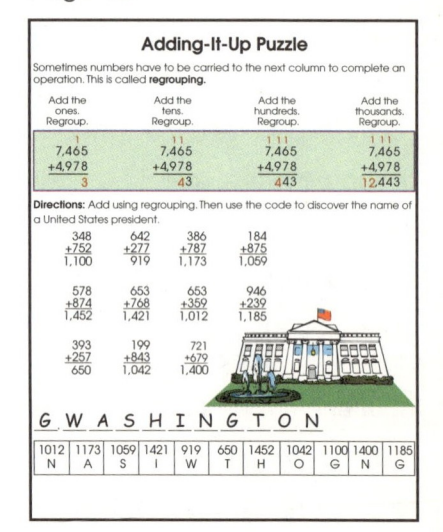

G W A S H I N G T O N

| 1012 | 1173 | 1059 | 1421 | 919 | 650 | 1452 | 1042 | 1100 | 1400 | 1185 |
| N | A | S | I | W | T | H | O | G | N | G |

Page 11
Scoreboard Subtraction
Subtraction means "taking away" or subtracting one number from another to find the difference. For example, 10 - 3 = 7. To regroup is to use one ten to form ten ones, one 100 to form ten tens and so on.

Directions: Study the example. Subtract using regrouping.

Example:
32 = 2 tens + 12 ones
-13 = 1 ten + 3 ones
19 = 1 ten + 9 ones

- 33 - 28 = 5
- 86 - 59 = 27
- 92 - 37 = 55
- 71 - 48 = 23
- 63 - 47 = 16
- 45 - 18 = 27
- 31 - 22 = 9
- 55 - 39 = 16
- 82 - 69 = **13**
- 73 - 36 = **37**

The Yankees won 85 games. The Cubs won 69 games. How many more games did the Yankees win? **16**

Page 12
Fancy Flower Subtraction
Directions: Regrouping for subtraction is the opposite of regrouping for addition. Study the example. Subtract using regrouping. Then use the code to color the flowers.

Example:
647
-453
194

Steps:
1. Subtract ones.
2. Subtract tens. Five tens cannot be subtracted from 4 tens.
3. Regroup tens by regrouping 6 hundreds (5 hundreds + 10 tens).
4. Add the 10 tens to the four tens.
5. Subtract 5 tens from 14 tens.
6. Subtract the hundreds.

If the answer has:
1 one, color it red;
8 ones, color it pink;
5 ones, color it yellow.

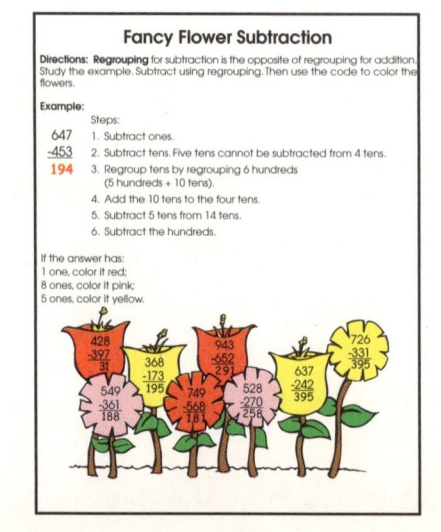

- 428 - 397 = 31; 549 - 361 = 188
- 368 - 173 = 195; 749 - 568 = 181
- 943 - 652 = 291; 528 - 270 = 258
- 637 - 242 = 395
- 726 - 331 = 395

Page 13
Problem Solving at the Fair
Directions: Read and solve each problem. Fill in the bubble next to the correct answer.

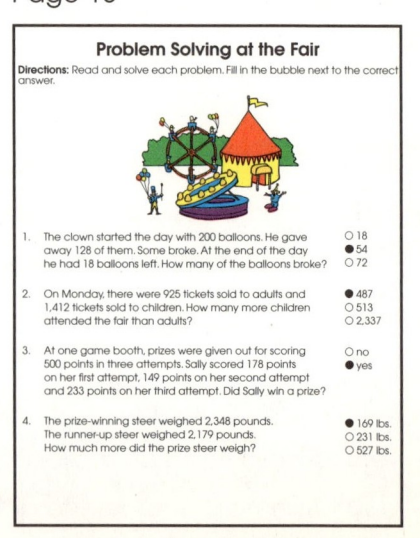

1. The clown started the day with 200 balloons. He gave away 128 of them. Some broke. At the end of the day he had 18 balloons left. How many of the balloons broke?
   - ○ 18
   - ● 54
   - ○ 72

2. On Monday, there were 925 tickets sold to adults and 1,412 tickets sold to children. How many more children attended the fair than adults?
   - ● 487
   - ○ 513
   - ○ 2,337

3. At one game booth, prizes were given out for scoring 500 points in three attempts. Sally scored 178 points on her first attempt, 149 points on her second attempt and 233 points on her third attempt. Did Sally win a prize?
   - ○ no
   - ● yes

4. The prize-winning steer weighed 2,348 pounds. The runner-up steer weighed 2,179 pounds. How much more did the prize steer weigh?
   - ● 169 lbs.
   - ○ 231 lbs.
   - ○ 527 lbs.

86

Summer Success

Page 14 — Multiplication Race

Multiplication means taking a number and adding it to itself a certain number of times.

Directions: Time yourself as you multiply. How quickly can you complete this page?

3 ×2 = 6	8 ×7 = 56	1 ×0 = 0	1 ×6 = 6	3 ×4 = 12	0 ×4 = 0
4 ×1 = 4	4 ×4 = 16	2 ×5 = 10	9 ×3 = 27	9 ×9 = 81	5 ×3 = 15
0 ×8 = 0	2 ×6 = 12	9 ×6 = 54	8 ×5 = 40	7 ×3 = 21	4 ×2 = 8
3 ×5 = 15	2 ×0 = 0	4 ×6 = 24	1 ×3 = 3	0 ×3 = 0	3 ×3 = 9

Page 15 — Amazing Arms

What will happen to a starfish that loses an arm? To find out, solve the following problems and write the matching letter above the answer at the bottom of the page.

O. 2,893 × 4 = 11,572
W. 1,763 × 3 = 5,289
W. 7,665 × 5 = 38,325

A. 1,935 × 6 = 11,610
W. 3,097 × 3 = 9,291
E. 2,929 × 4 = 11,716

G. 6,366 × 5 = 31,830
T. 7,821 × 8 = 62,568
L. 6,283 × 7 = 43,981
I. 5,257 × 3 = 15,771
R. 3,019 × 6 = 18,114

N. 2,908 × 7 = 20,356
I. 6,507 × 8 = 52,056
N. 5,527 × 2 = 11,054

L. 6,626 × 3 = 19,878
O. 7,219 × 9 = 64,971
E. 3,406 × 6 = 20,436

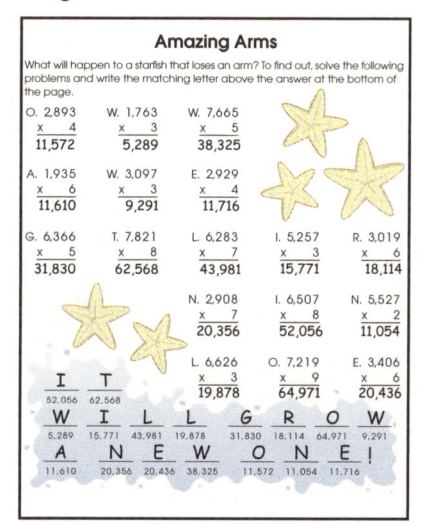

I T W I L L G R O W   A N E W O N E!
52,056 62,568   5,289 15,771 19,878 43,981 31,830 64,971 11,610   9,291 11,054 20,436 38,325   11,572 11,054 11,716

Page 16 — Multiplication Puzzles With Regrouping

Example:
Steps:
Multiply by the ones. Carry numbers as needed.
6,074 × 38 → 48,592

Multiply by the tens. Carry numbers as needed. Put a zero in the ones place.
6,074 × 38 → 182,220

Add.
48,592 + 182,220 = 230,612

Directions: Multiply along each diagonal of the square. Write the answer in the oval.

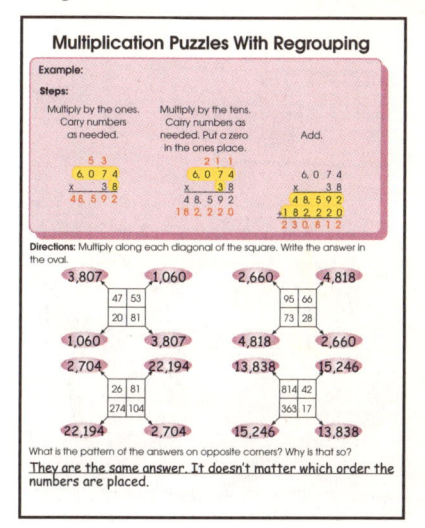

3,807 — 47 53 — 1,060
       20 81
1,060 — 3,807
2,704 — 26 81 — 22,194
       274 104
22,194 — 2,704

2,660 — 95 66 — 4,818
        73 28
4,818 — 2,660
13,838 — 814 42 — 15,246
         363 17
15,246 — 13,838

What is the pattern of the answers on opposite corners? Why is that so?
They are the same answer. It doesn't matter which order the numbers are placed.

Page 17 — Match the Sail

Division shows how many times one number contains another.

Directions: Divide. Draw a line from the boat to the sail with the correct answer. The first one has been done for you.

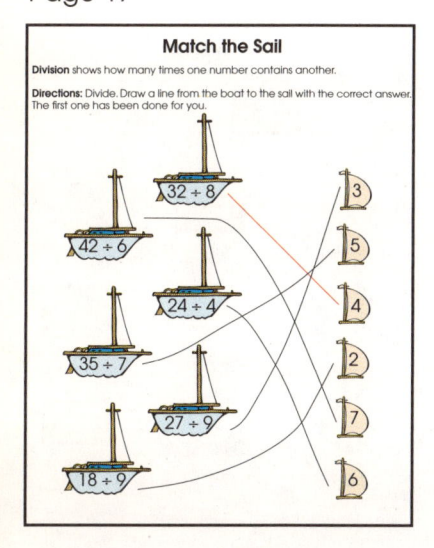

- 32 ÷ 8 → 3
- 42 ÷ 6 → 5
- 24 ÷ 4 → 4
- 35 ÷ 7 → 2
- 27 ÷ 9 → 7
- 18 ÷ 9 → 6

Page 18 — Division Drop In

Directions: What does dropping in mean to a skateboarder? To find out, solve each division problem. Then, write the matching letter above the answer below.

O. 4)356 = 89
T. 6)246 = 41
P. 9)684 = 76
T. 3)525 = 175
R. 6)930 = 155
A. 4)392 = 98
H. 3)291 = 97
P. 8)496 = 62
T. 3)201 = 67
E. 7)448 = 64
S. 5)375 = 75
T. 9)648 = 72
F. 6)294 = 49
T. 6)192 = 32
R. 2)730 = 365
A. 5)385 = 77
M. 4)292 = 73

T O   S T A R T   A T   T H E   T O P   O F   A   R A M P
175 89   175 41 98 365 67   41 73   175 97 62   175 67 76   67 41   98   365 98 64 76   89 49   98   155 77 73 76

Page 19 — On the Road

The Olympics are held in a different international city every time. All athletes must travel to play or compete.

Directions: Your bags are packed with division problems. Solve these problems.

Steps for division:
1. Divide.
2. Multiply.
3. Subtract.
4. Bring down.
5. Go back to step 1 or add the remainder.

Example: 4)19 = 4r3, 16, 3

- 8)55 = 6R7
- 9)63 = 7
- 5)29 = 5R4
- 8)30 = 3R6
- 7)24 = 4R6

(6)24 = 4
3)7 = 2R1
6)53 = 8R5
2)11 = 5R1
7)40 = 5R5
6)22 = 3R4
6 = 6
8)44 = 5R4
5)33 = 6R3
3)17 = 5R2

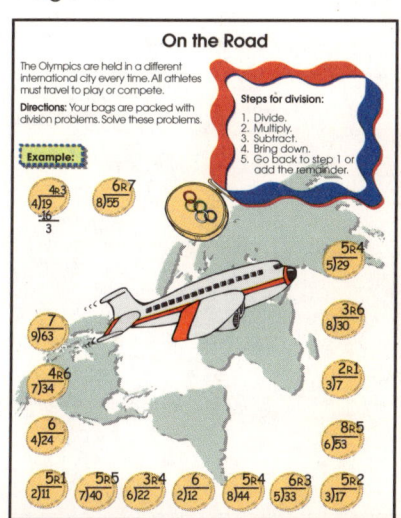

Page 20 — Problem Solving in the Garden

Directions: Read and solve each problem using either multiplication or division.

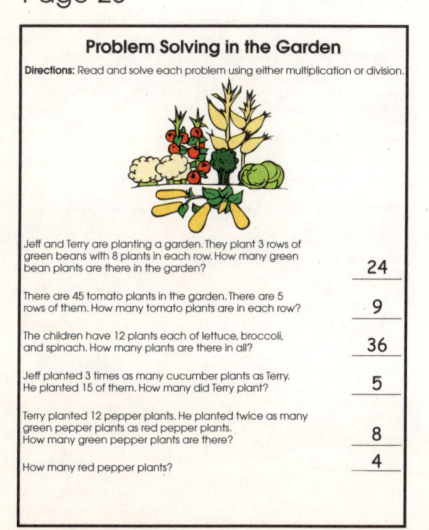

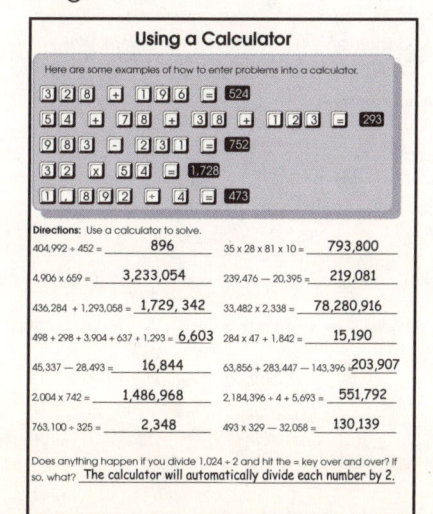

Jeff and Terry are planting a garden. They plant 3 rows of green beans with 8 plants in each row. How many green bean plants are there in the garden? **24**

There are 45 tomato plants in the garden. There are 5 rows of them. How many tomato plants are in each row? **9**

The children have 12 plants each of lettuce, broccoli, and spinach. How many plants are there in all? **36**

Jeff planted 3 times as many cucumber plants as Terry. He planted 15 of them. How many did Terry plant? **5**

Terry planted 12 pepper plants. He planted twice as many green pepper plants as red pepper plants. How many green pepper plants are there? **8**

How many red pepper plants? **4**

Page 21 — Using a Calculator

Here are some examples of how to enter problems into a calculator.

328 + 196 = 524
54 + 78 + 38 + 123 = 293
983 − 231 = 752
32 × 54 = 1,728
1,892 ÷ 4 = 473

Directions: Use a calculator to solve.

404,992 ÷ 452 = **896**
35 × 28 × 81 × 10 = **793,800**
4,906 × 659 = **3,233,054**
239,476 − 20,395 = **219,081**
436,284 + 1,293,058 = **1,729,342**
33,482 × 2,338 = **78,280,916**
498 + 298 + 3,904 + 637 + 1,293 = **6,603**
284 × 47 + 1,842 = **15,190**
45,337 − 28,493 = **16,844**
63,856 + 283,447 − 143,396 = **203,907**
2,004 × 742 = **1,486,968**
2,184,396 ÷ 4 + 5,693 = **551,792**
763,100 ÷ 325 = **2,348**
493 × 329 − 32,058 = **130,139**

Does anything happen if you divide 1,024 ÷ 2 and hit the = key over and over? If so, what? **The calculator will automatically divide each number by 2.**

Page 22 — The Order of Things

When you solve a problem that involves more than one operation, this is the order to follow, known as the **Order of Operations**.

( ) Parentheses first
×   Multiplication
÷   Division
+   Addition
−   Subtraction

Example:
2 + (3 × 5) − 2 = 15
17 − 2 = 15

Directions: Solve the problems using the correct order of operations or use +, −, ×, and ÷ to complete the problems so the number sentence is true.

(5 − 3) + 4 × 7 = **30**
9 + **_3_** − 9 = 3

(8 **_÷_** 2) + 4 = 8
1 + 2 × 3 + 4 = **11**

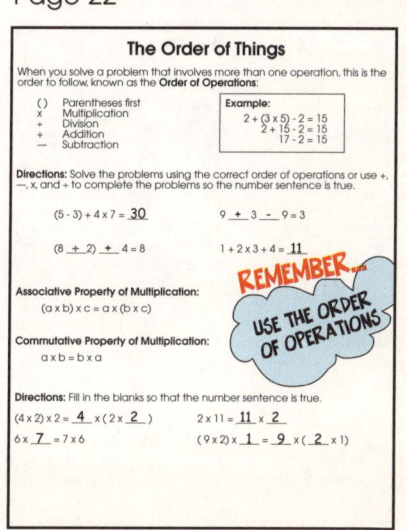

Associative Property of Multiplication:
(a × b) × c = a × (b × c)

Commutative Property of Multiplication:
a × b = b × a

REMEMBER... USE THE ORDER OF OPERATIONS

Directions: Fill in the blanks so that the number sentence is true.

(4 × 2) × 2 = **_4_** × (2 × **_2_**)
2 × 11 = **_11_** × **_2_**
6 × **_7_** = 7 × 6
(9 × 2) × **_1_** = **_9_** × (**_2_** × 1)

87

SUMMER SUCCESS

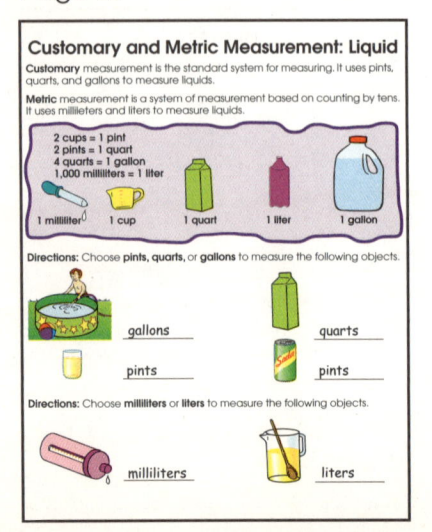

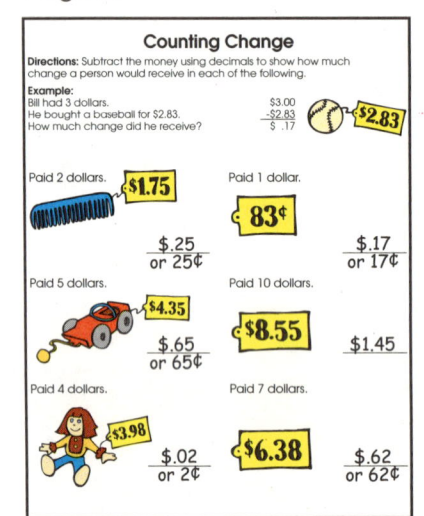

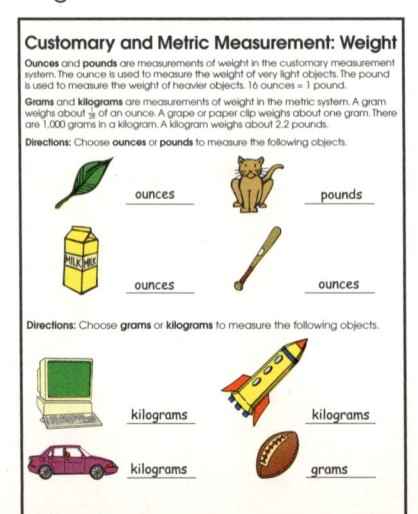

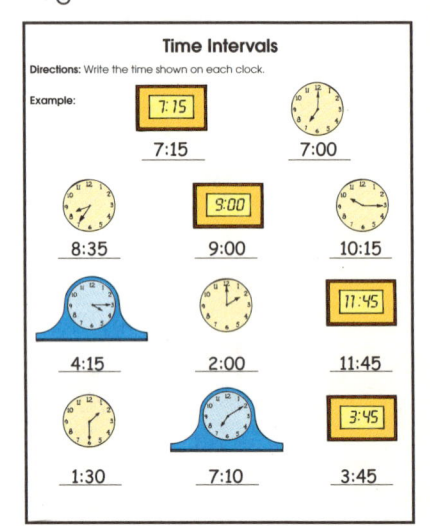

Page 23: Flourishing Fractions

The bottom number in a fraction, telling the number of parts in the whole, is called a **denominator**. The **numerator** is the top part of a fraction that shows the number of parts out of the whole.

When adding fractions with the same denominator, the denominator stays the same. Add only the numerators.

Example: $\frac{\text{numerator}}{\text{denominator}}\quad \frac{1}{8} + \frac{2}{8} = \frac{3}{8}$

Directions: Add the fractions on the flowers. Begin in the center of each flower and add each petal. The first one is done for you.

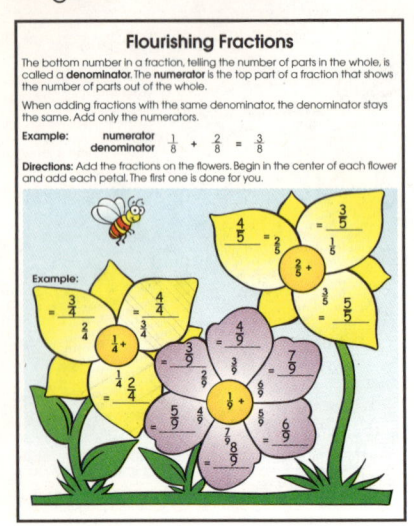

Page 24: Falling Fractions

When subtracting fractions with the same denominator, the denominator stays the same. Subtract only the numerators.

Directions: Solve the problems, working from left to right. As you find each answer, copy the letter from the key into the numbered blanks. The answer is the name of a famous American. The first one is done for you.

1. $\frac{3}{8} - \frac{2}{8} = \frac{1}{8}$
2. $\frac{2}{4} - \frac{1}{4} = \frac{1}{4}$
3. $\frac{5}{9} - \frac{3}{9} = \frac{2}{9}$
4. $\frac{2}{3} - \frac{1}{3} = \frac{1}{3}$
5. $\frac{8}{12} - \frac{7}{12} = \frac{1}{12}$
6. $\frac{4}{5} - \frac{1}{5} = \frac{3}{5}$
7. $\frac{6}{12} - \frac{3}{12} = \frac{3}{12}$
8. $\frac{4}{9} - \frac{1}{9} = \frac{3}{9}$
9. $\frac{11}{12} - \frac{7}{12} = \frac{4}{12}$
10. $\frac{7}{8} - \frac{3}{8} = \frac{4}{8}$
11. $\frac{4}{7} - \frac{2}{7} = \frac{2}{7}$
12. $\frac{14}{16} - \frac{7}{16} = \frac{7}{16}$
13. $\frac{18}{20} - \frac{13}{20} = \frac{5}{20}$
14. $\frac{13}{15} - \frac{2}{15} = \frac{11}{15}$
15. $\frac{5}{6} - \frac{3}{6} = \frac{2}{6}$

Who helped write the Declaration of Independence?

T H O M A S   J E F F E R S O N

Page 25: Starting Points

A **decimal** is a number with one or more numbers to the right of a decimal point. A **decimal point** is a dot placed between the ones place and the tens place of a number, such as 2.5.

Decimals are added and subtracted in the same way as other numbers. Simply carry down the decimal point to your answer.

Directions: Add or subtract.

Examples:
1.3 + 2.8 = 4.1
4.5 − 2.2 = 2.3

1.3 + 2.2 = 3.5
4.6 − 3.4 = 1.2
5.1 + 8.8 = 13.9
6.7 − 4.3 = 2.4

7.9 − 3.7 = 4.2
6.4 + 8.7 = 15.1
11.4 − 9.5 = 1.9
0.5 + 3.6 = 4.1

9.3 + 1.2 = 10.5
2.5 − 0.7 = 1.8
1.2 + 5.0 = 6.2

Bob jogs around the school every day. The distance for one time around is .7 of a mile. If he jogs around the school two times, how many miles does he jog each day? **1.4**

Page 26: A Money Message

Directions: What's the smartest thing to do with your money? To find out, solve the following problems and write the matching letter above the answer.

S A V E   I T ,
A N D   I T   W I L L
A D D   U P !

V = $42.13 + 8.29 = $50.42
A = $4.56 + 29.38 = $33.94
N = $4.65 + 21.48 = $26.13
S = $23.46 + 19.25 = $42.71

P = $9.31 + 33.48 = $42.79
L = $6.73 + 4.28 = $11.01
E = $81.49 + 19.24 = $100.73
T = $.42 + 1.94 + .03 = $2.39

U = $50.84 + 4.92 = $55.76
I = $7.49 + 38.21 = $45.70

D = $3.04 + 84.98 = $88.02
W = $1.89 + 49.23 = $51.12

Page 27: Counting Change

Directions: Subtract the money using decimals to show how much change a person would receive in each of the following.

Example:
Bill had 3 dollars. He bought a baseball for $2.83. How much change did he receive?
$3.00 − $2.83 = $.17

Paid 2 dollars. $1.75 → $.25 or 25¢
Paid 1 dollar. 83¢ → $.17 or 17¢
Paid 5 dollars. $4.35 → $.65 or 65¢
Paid 10 dollars. $8.55 → $1.45
Paid 4 dollars. $3.98 → $.02 or 2¢
Paid 7 dollars. $6.38 → $.62 or 62¢

Page 28: Time Intervals

Directions: Write the time shown on each clock.

Example: 7:15

7:15, 7:00, 8:35, 9:00, 10:15, 4:15, 2:00, 11:45, 1:30, 7:10, 3:45

Page 29: Customary and Metric Measurement: Liquid

Customary measurement is the standard system for measuring. It uses pints, quarts, and gallons to measure liquids.

Metric measurement is a system of measurement based on counting by tens. It uses milliliters and liters to measure liquids.

2 cups = 1 pint
2 pints = 1 quart
4 quarts = 1 gallon
1,000 milliliters = 1 liter

Directions: Choose **pints, quarts,** or **gallons** to measure the following objects.
gallons, quarts, pints, pints

Directions: Choose **milliliters** or **liters** to measure the following objects.
milliliters, liters

Page 30: Customary and Metric Measurement: Weight

Ounces and **pounds** are measurements of weight in the customary measurement system. The ounce is used to measure the weight of very light objects. The pound is used to measure the weight of heavier objects. 16 ounces = 1 pound.

Grams and **kilograms** are measurements of weight in the metric system. A gram weighs about 1/28 of an ounce. A grape or paper clip weighs about one gram. There are 1,000 grams in a kilogram. A kilogram weighs about 2.2 pounds.

Directions: Choose **ounces** or **pounds** to measure the following objects.
ounces, pounds, ounces, ounces

Directions: Choose **grams** or **kilograms** to measure the following objects.
kilograms, kilograms, kilograms, grams

Page 31: Customary and Metric Measurement: Distance

Feet, yards, and **miles** are units of length in the customary system. A foot is equal to 12 inches. A yard is equal to 3 feet. A mile is equal to 1,760 yards.

Directions: Decide whether you would use **foot, yard,** or **mile** to measure each object.
length of a river __mile__ width of a room __foot__
height of a tree __yard or foot__ length of a football field __yard__

Meters and **kilometers** are units of length in the metric system. A meter is equal to 39.37 inches. A kilometer is equal to about 5/8 of a mile.

Directions: Decide whether you would use **meter** or **kilometer** to measure each object.
height of a door __meter__ length of a race __meter or kilometer__
length of a dress __meter__ height of a basketball pole __meter__

1 foot = 12 inches
1 yard = 36 inches or 3 feet
1 mile = 1,760 yards
1 meter = 100 centimeters
1 kilometer = 1,000 meters

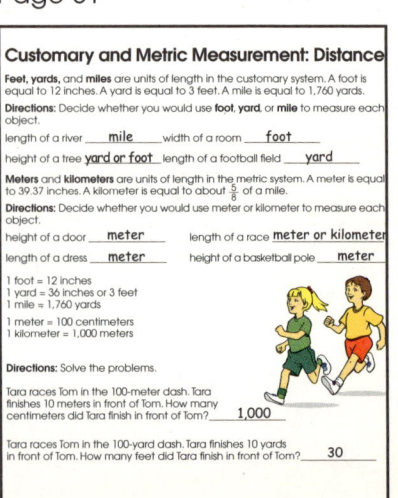

Directions: Solve the problems.

Tara races Tom in the 100-meter dash. Tara finishes 10 meters in front of Tom. How many centimeters did Tara finish in front of Tom? __1,000__

Tara races Tom in the 100-yard dash. Tara finishes 10 yards in front of Tom. How many feet did Tara finish in front of Tom? __30__

SUMMER SUCCESS

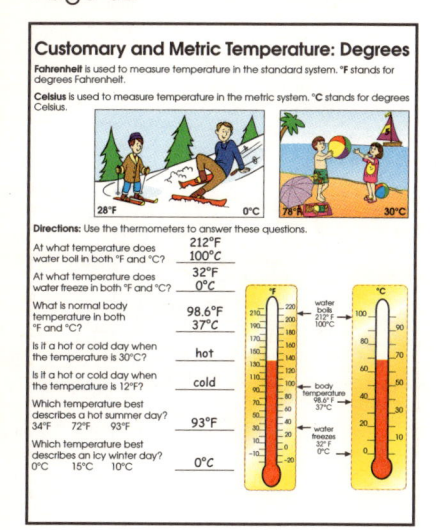

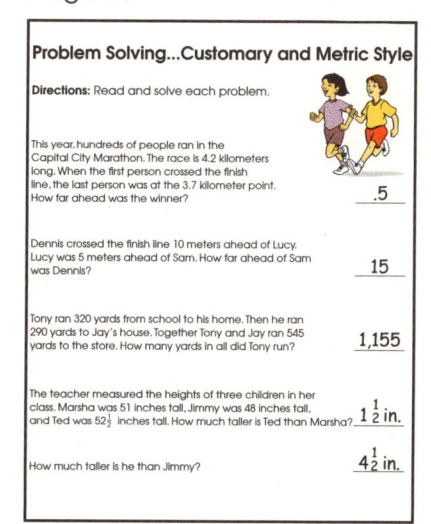

Page 32
Customary and Metric Temperature: Degrees
Fahrenheit is used to measure temperature in the standard system. °F stands for degrees Fahrenheit.
Celsius is used to measure temperature in the metric system. °C stands for degrees Celsius.

Directions: Use the thermometers to answer these questions.

At what temperature does water boil in both °F and °C?	212°F / 100°C
At what temperature does water freeze in both °F and °C?	32°F / 0°C
What is normal body temperature in both °F and °C?	98.6°F / 37°C
Is it a hot or cold day when the temperature is 30°C?	hot
Is it a hot or cold day when the temperature is 12°F?	cold
Which temperature best describes a hot summer day? 34°F 72°F 93°F	93°F
Which temperature best describes an icy winter day? 0°C 15°C 10°C	0°C

Page 33
Problem Solving...Customary and Metric Style
Directions: Read and solve each problem.

This year, hundreds of people ran in the Capital City Marathon. The race is 4.2 kilometers long. When the first person crossed the finish line, the last person was at the 3.7 kilometer point. How far ahead was the winner? **.5**

Dennis crossed the finish line 10 meters ahead of Lucy. Lucy was 5 meters ahead of Sam. How far ahead of Sam was Dennis? **15**

Tony ran 320 yards from school to his home. Then he ran 290 yards to Jay's house. Together Tony and Jay ran 545 yards to the store. How many yards in all did Tony run? **1,155**

The teacher measured the heights of three children in her class. Marsha was 51 inches tall, Jimmy was 48 inches tall, and Ted was 52½ inches tall. How much taller is Ted than Marsha? **1½ in.**

How much taller is he than Jimmy? **4½ in.**

Page 34
Finding Your Way Around
The **perimeter** is the distance around an object. Find the perimeter by adding the lengths of all the sides.
Directions: Find the perimeter for each object (ft. = feet). The first one is done for you.

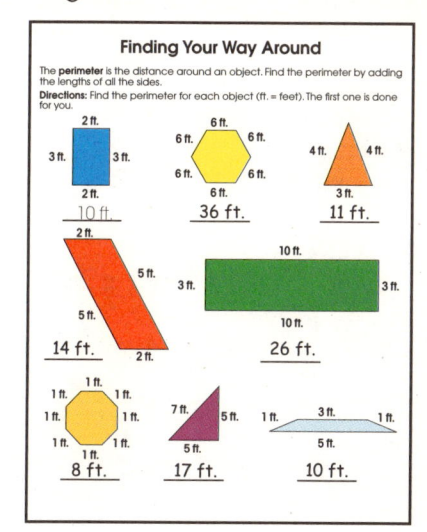

- Square (2 ft sides): **10 ft**
- Hexagon (6 ft sides): **36 ft**
- Triangle (4 ft sides): **11 ft**
- Parallelogram (2 ft, 5 ft): **14 ft**
- Rectangle (10 ft, 3 ft): **26 ft**
- Octagon (1 ft sides): **8 ft**
- Pentagon (7 ft, 5 ft): **17 ft**
- Quadrilateral: **10 ft**

Page 35
Cover the Area
The Local Area Construction Company has been hired by the city to build a recreation center. They will construct a baseball diamond, a basketball court, and a tennis court. How many square feet of land do they need in order to complete each structure? When you want to know the amount of surface in a given boundary, you need to multiply the length by the width. This is called the **area**.

Directions: Find the area of each figure below. (Area = L × W)
Area = square feet

- Tennis court (78 × 36): Area = **2,808 sq. ft.**
- Baseball diamond (90 × 90): Area = **8,100 sq. ft.**
- Basketball court (94 × 50): Area = **4,700 sq. ft.**

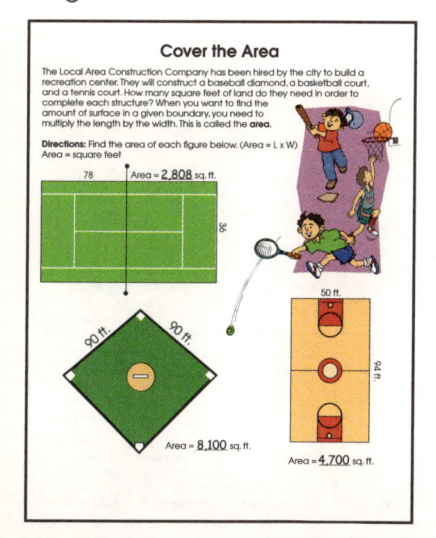

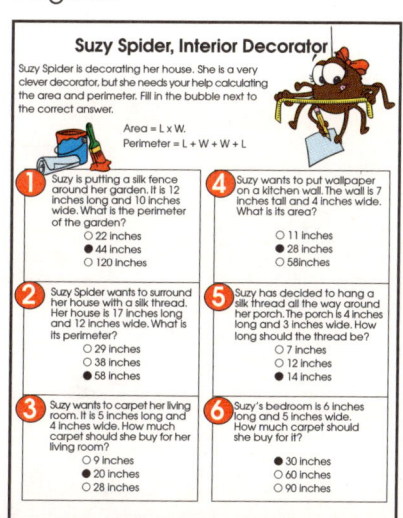

Page 36
Suzy Spider, Interior Decorator
Suzy Spider is decorating her house. She is a very clever decorator, but she needs your help calculating the area and perimeter. Fill in the bubble next to the correct answer.

Area = L × W.
Perimeter = L + W + W + L

1. Suzy is putting a silk fence around her garden. It is 12 inches long and 10 inches wide. What is the perimeter of the garden?
 - 22 inches
 - ● 44 inches
 - 120 inches

2. Suzy Spider wants to surround her house with a silk thread. Her house is 17 inches long and 12 inches wide. What is its perimeter?
 - 29 inches
 - 38 inches
 - ● 58 inches

3. Suzy wants to carpet her living room. It is 5 inches long and 4 inches wide. How much carpet should she buy for her living room?
 - 9 inches
 - ● 20 inches
 - 28 inches

4. Suzy wants to put wallpaper on a kitchen wall. The wall is 7 inches tall and 4 inches wide. What is its area?
 - 11 inches
 - ● 28 inches
 - 58 inches

5. Suzy has decided to hang a silk thread all the way around her porch. The porch is 4 inches long and 3 inches wide. How long should the thread be?
 - 7 inches
 - 12 inches
 - ● 14 inches

6. Suzy's bedroom is 6 inches long and 5 inches wide. How much carpet should she buy for it?
 - ● 30 inches
 - 60 inches
 - 90 inches

Page 37
Pattern Maze
Directions: Follow the pattern ● ■ ▲ ★ to get through the maze.

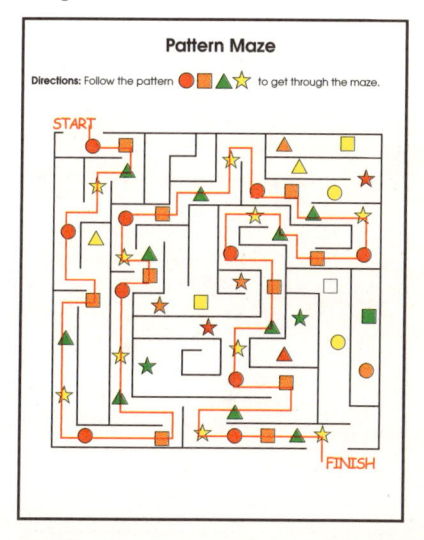

START ... FINISH

Page 38
Set! Point! Match!
Polygon: A closed figure made with line segments that are joined together.
Triangle: A three-sided polygon.
Square: A figure with four equal sides and four 90 degree angles.
Trapezoid: A polygon with four sides and exactly two sides parallel.
Rectangle: A four-sided polygon with four 90 degree angles.
Parallelogram: A four-sided polygon with opposite sides parallel.
Rhombus: A parallelogram with equal sides.

Directions: Match each polygon to its name.

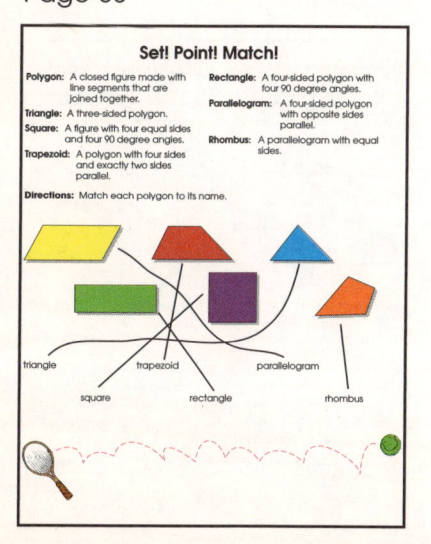

triangle, trapezoid, parallelogram, square, rectangle, rhombus

Page 39
Comparing Polygons
Directions: Choose two of the figures from page 38. Complete the Venn diagram below by comparing the two polygons.

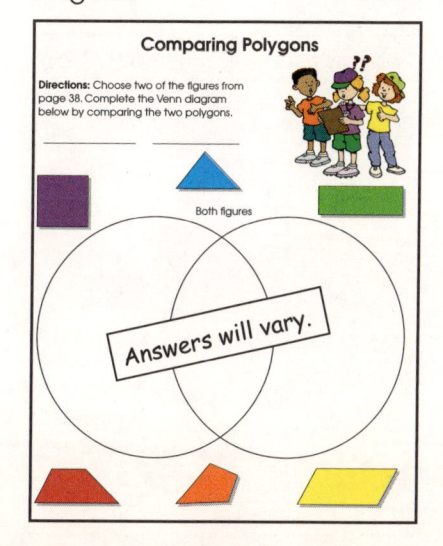

Both figures

Answers will vary.

Page 40
Geometry
Geometry is the branch of mathematics that has to do with points, lines, and shapes.

cube — rectangular prism — cone — cylinder — sphere

Directions: Use the code to color the picture.

Color:
cubes — blue
rectangular prisms — red
cones — green
cylinders — yellow
spheres — orange

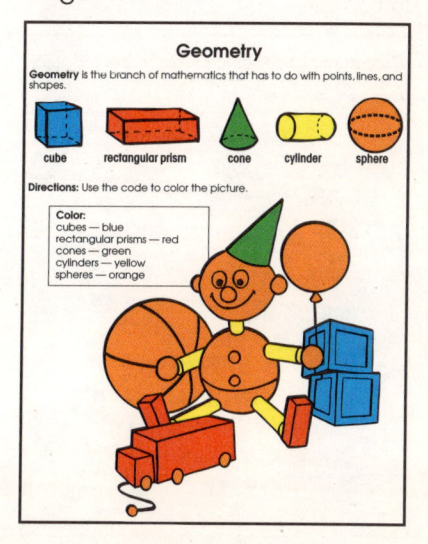

89

SUMMER SUCCESS

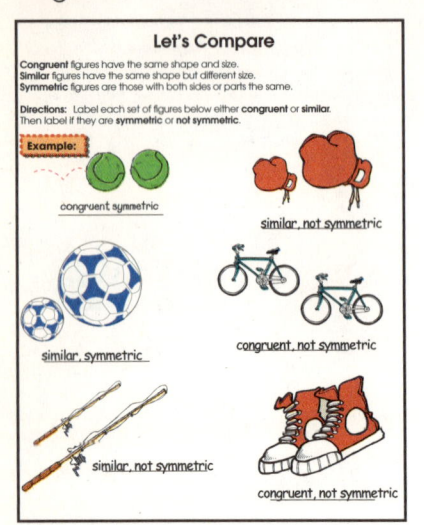

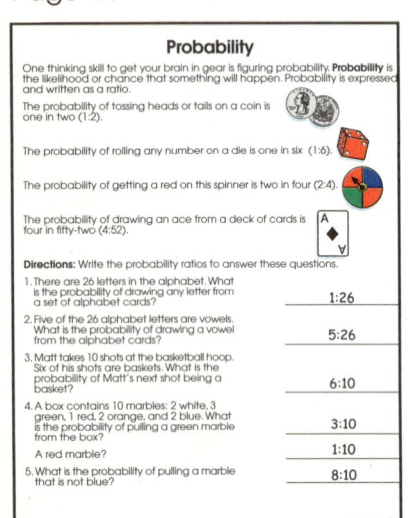

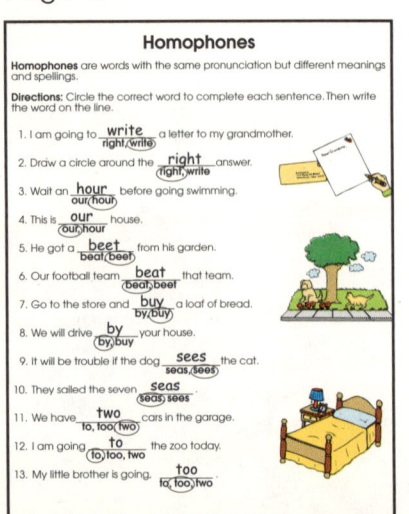

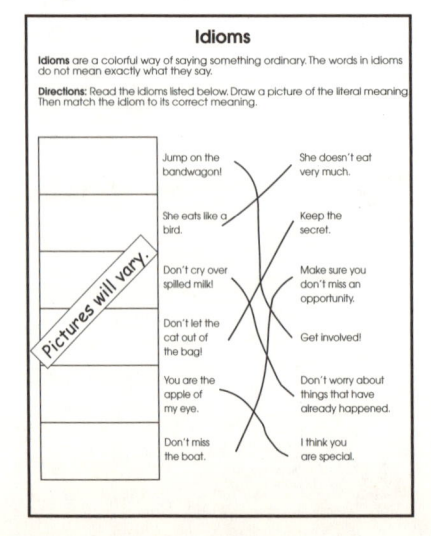

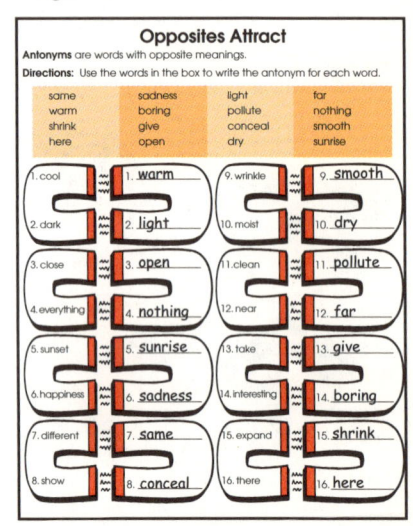

Page 41: Let's Compare

Congruent figures have the same shape and size.
Similar figures have the same shape but different size.
Symmetric figures are those with both sides or parts the same.

Directions: Label each set of figures below either congruent or similar. Then label if they are symmetric or not symmetric.

Example: congruent symmetric
- similar, not symmetric
- similar, symmetric
- congruent, not symmetric
- similar, not symmetric
- congruent, not symmetric

Page 42: Candy Sales

Every year the students at Lincoln Elementary sell candy as a fund-raising project. These are the results of the sales for this year. They can show their sales on a **bar graph**, which displays information by lengths of parallel rectangular bars.

Grade Level	Number of Sales
Kindergarten	40
First	70
Second	50
Third	80
Fourth	85
Fifth	75

Directions: Color the bar graph to show the number of sales made at each grade level.

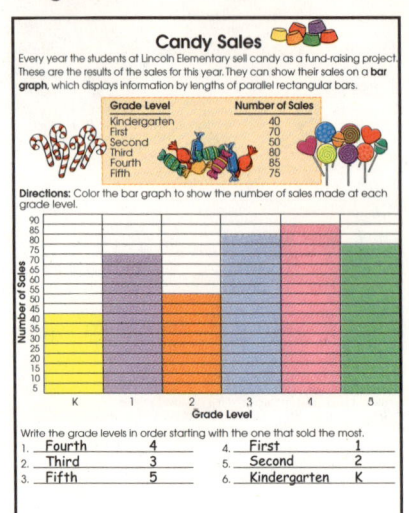

Write the grade levels in order starting with the one that sold the most.
1. Fourth — 4
2. Third — 3
3. Fifth — 5
4. First — 1
5. Second — 2
6. Kindergarten — K

Page 43: Coordinating Coordinates

Coordinates are points located on a graph.
Directions: Locate the points on the grid and color in each box.

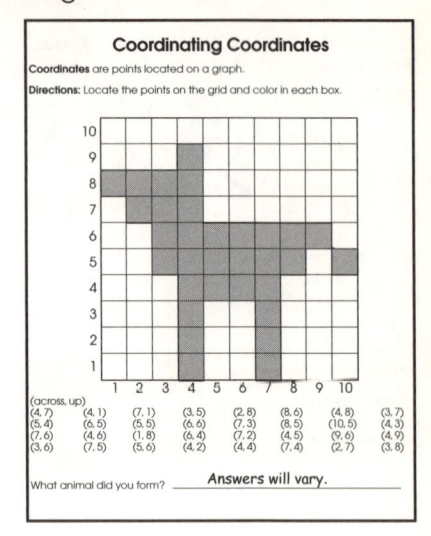

(across, up)
(4,7) (4,1) (7,1) (3,5) (2,8) (8,6) (4,8) (3,7)
(5,4) (6,5) (5,5) (6,6) (7,3) (8,5) (10,5) (4,3)
(7,6) (4,6) (1,8) (6,4) (7,2) (4,5) (9,6) (4,9)
(3,6) (7,5) (5,6) (4,2) (4,4) (7,4) (2,7) (3,8)

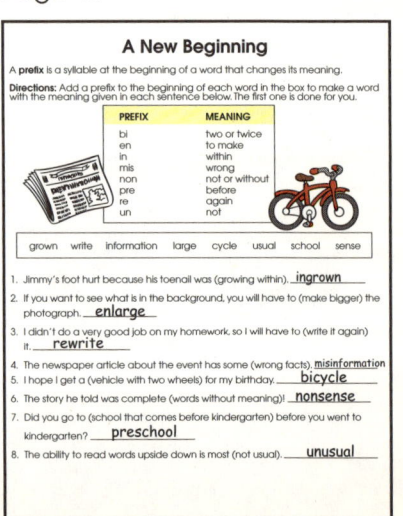

What animal did you form? _Answers will vary._

Page 44: Probability

One thinking skill to get your brain in gear is figuring probability. **Probability** is the likelihood or chance that something will happen. Probability is expressed as a ratio.

The probability of tossing heads or tails on a coin is one in two (1:2).

The probability of rolling any number on a die is one in six (1:6).

The probability of getting a red on this spinner is two in four (2:4).

The probability of drawing an ace from a deck of cards is four in fifty-two (4:52).

Directions: Write the probability ratios to answer these questions.

1. There are 26 letters in the alphabet. What is the probability of drawing any letter from a set of alphabet cards? — **1:26**
2. Five of the 26 alphabet letters are vowels. What is the probability of drawing a vowel from the alphabet cards? — **5:26**
3. Matt takes 10 shots at the basketball hoop. Six of his shots are baskets. What is the probability of Matt's next shot being a basket? — **6:10**
4. A box contains 10 marbles: 2 white, 3 green, 1 red, 2 orange, and 2 blue. What is the probability of pulling a green marble from the box? — **3:10**
   A red marble? — **1:10**
5. What is the probability of pulling a marble that is not blue? — **8:10**

Page 45: Synonyms Riddle

Synonyms are words that mean the same, or almost the same, thing.
Directions: Write a word from the box that is a synonym for each word.

evening, heat, eat, prepare, guess, fuss, wish, relax, explain, glance

1. worry — f u s s
2. estimate — g u e s s
3. night — e v e n i n g
4. devour — e a t
5. make — p r e p a r e
6. warm — h e a t
7. clarify — e x p l a i n
8. look — g l a n c e
9. desire — w i s h
10. rest — r e l a x

Directions: Use the letters in the triangles to answer the riddle. (Hint: Read down.)

Tommy: My pen just fell down the drain. What should I do?
Harold: U s e   a   p e n c i l !

Page 46: Opposites Attract

Antonyms are words with opposite meanings.
Directions: Use the words in the box to write the antonym for each word.

same, sadness, light, far, warm, boring, pollute, nothing, shrink, give, conceal, smooth, here, open, dry, sunrise

1. cool — warm
2. dark — light
3. close — open
4. everything — nothing
5. sunset — sunrise
6. happiness — sadness
7. different — same
8. show — conceal
9. wrinkle — smooth
10. moist — dry
11. clean — pollute
12. near — far
13. take — give
14. interesting — boring
15. expand — shrink
16. there — here

Page 47: Homophones

Homophones are words with the same pronunciation but different meanings and spellings.
Directions: Circle the correct word to complete each sentence. Then write the word on the line.

1. I am going to **write** a letter to my grandmother. (right, write)
2. Draw a circle around the **right** answer. (right, write)
3. Wait an **hour** before going swimming. (our, hour)
4. This is **our** house. (our, hour)
5. He got a **beet** from his garden. (beat, beet)
6. Our football team **beat** that team. (beat, beet)
7. Go to the store and **buy** a loaf of bread. (by, buy)
8. We will drive **by** your house. (by, buy)
9. It will be trouble if the dog **sees** the cat. (seas, sees)
10. They sailed the seven **seas**. (seas, sees)
11. We have **two** cars in the garage. (to, too, two)
12. I am going **to** the zoo today. (to, too, two)
13. My little brother is going, **too**. (to, too, two)

Page 48: Idioms

Idioms are a colorful way of saying something ordinary. The words in idioms do not mean exactly what they say.
Directions: Read the idioms listed below. Draw a picture of the literal meaning. Then match the idiom to its correct meaning.

Pictures will vary.

- Jump on the bandwagon! — Get involved!
- She eats like a bird. — She doesn't eat very much.
- Don't cry over spilled milk! — Don't worry about things that have already happened.
- Don't let the cat out of the bag! — Keep the secret.
- You are the apple of my eye. — I think you are special.
- Don't miss the boat. — Make sure you don't miss an opportunity.

Page 49: A New Beginning

A **prefix** is a syllable at the beginning of a word that changes its meaning.
Directions: Add a prefix to the beginning of each word in the box to make a word with the meaning given in each sentence below. The first one is done for you.

PREFIX	MEANING
bi	two or twice
en	to make
in	within
mis	wrong
non	not or without
pre	before
re	again
un	not

grown, write, information, large, cycle, usual, school, sense

1. Jimmy's foot hurt because his toenail was (growing within). **ingrown**
2. If you want to see what is in the background, you will have to (make bigger) the photograph. **enlarge**
3. I didn't do a very good job on my homework, so I will have to (write it again) it. **rewrite**
4. The newspaper article about the event has some (wrong facts). **misinformation**
5. I hope I get a (vehicle with two wheels) for my birthday. **bicycle**
6. The story he told was complete (words without meaning)! **nonsense**
7. Did you go to (school that comes before kindergarten) before you went to kindergarten? **preschool**
8. The ability to read words upside down is most (not usual). **unusual**

SUMMER SUCCESS

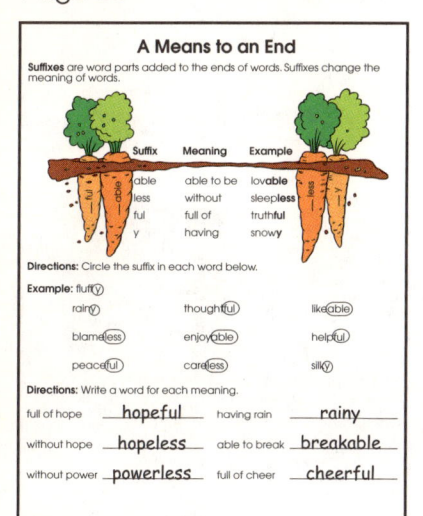

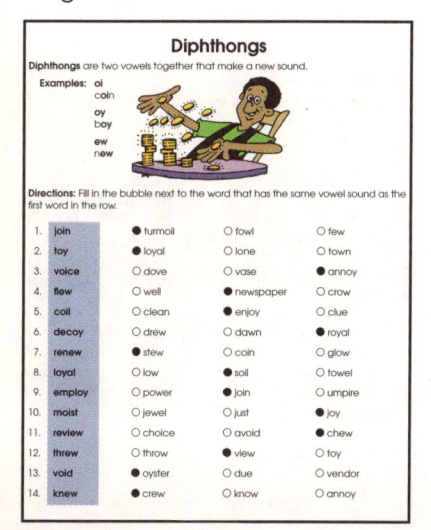

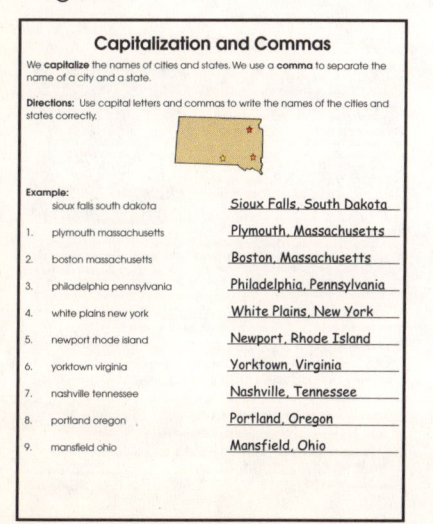

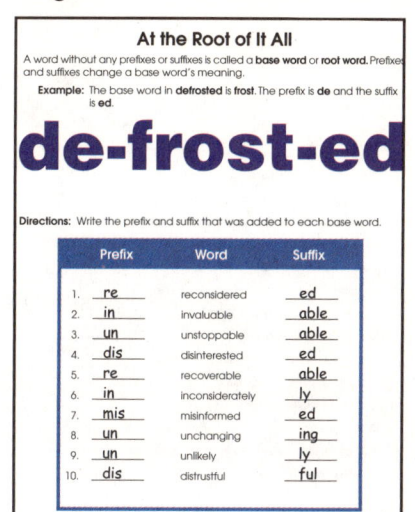

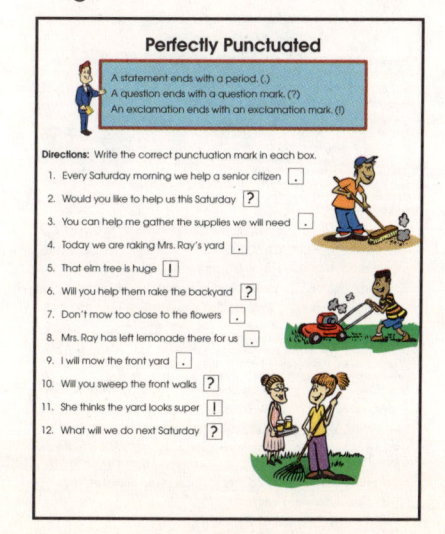

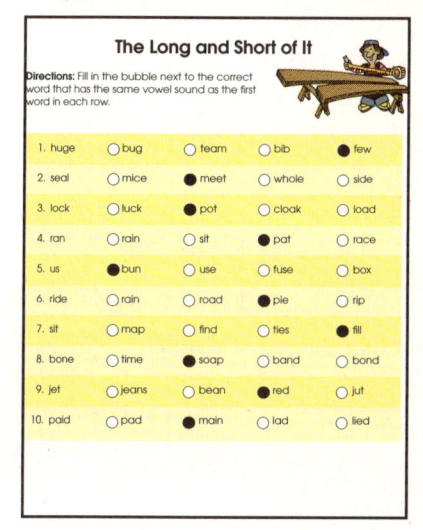

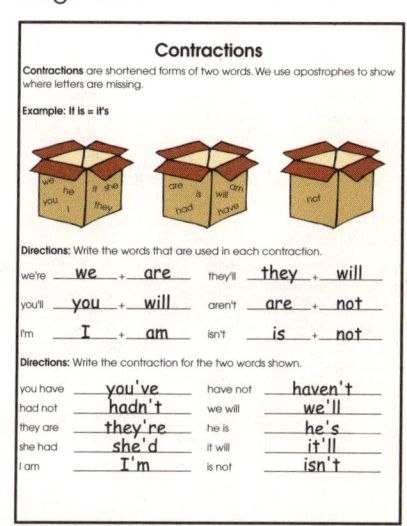

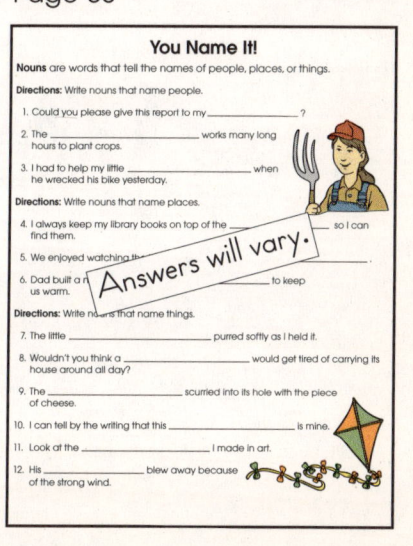

Page 50 — A Means to an End

Suffixes are word parts added to the ends of words. Suffixes change the meaning of words.

Suffix	Meaning	Example
able	able to be	lovable
less	without	sleepless
ful	full of	truthful
y	having	snowy

Directions: Circle the suffix in each word below.

Example: fluff**y**

- rain**y**
- thought**ful**
- lik**able**
- blame**less**
- enjoy**able**
- help**ful**
- peace**ful**
- care**less**
- sill**y**

Directions: Write a word for each meaning.

- full of hope — **hopeful**
- having rain — **rainy**
- without hope — **hopeless**
- able to break — **breakable**
- without power — **powerless**
- full of cheer — **cheerful**

Page 51 — At the Root of It All

A word without any prefixes or suffixes is called a **base word** or **root word**. Prefixes and suffixes change a base word's meaning.

Example: The base word in **defrosted** is **frost**. The prefix is **de** and the suffix is **ed**.

de-frost-ed

Directions: Write the prefix and suffix that was added to each base word.

	Prefix	Word	Suffix
1.	re	reconsidered	ed
2.	in	invaluable	able
3.	un	unstoppable	able
4.	dis	disinterested	ed
5.	re	recoverable	able
6.	in	inconsiderately	ly
7.	mis	misinformed	ed
8.	un	unchanging	ing
9.	un	unlikely	ly
10.	dis	distrustful	ful

Page 52 — The Long and Short of It

Directions: Fill in the bubble next to the correct word that has the same vowel sound as the first word in each row.

1. huge	○ bug	○ team	○ bib	● few
2. seal	○ mice	● meet	○ whole	○ side
3. lock	○ luck	● pot	○ cloak	○ load
4. ran	○ rain	○ sit	● pat	○ race
5. us	● bun	○ use	○ fuse	○ box
6. ride	○ rain	○ road	● pie	○ rip
7. sit	○ map	○ find	○ ties	● fill
8. bone	○ time	● soap	○ band	○ bond
9. jet	○ jeans	● bean	○ red	○ jut
10. paid	○ pad	● main	○ lad	○ lied

Page 53 — Diphthongs

Diphthongs are two vowels together that make a new sound.

Examples: oi (coin), oy (boy), ew (new)

Directions: Fill in the bubble next to the word that has the same vowel sound as the first word in the row.

1. join	● turmoil	○ fowl	○ few
2. toy	○ loyal	○ lone	○ town
3. voice	○ dove	○ vase	● annoy
4. flew	○ well	● newspaper	○ crow
5. coil	○ clean	○ enjoy	○ clue
6. decoy	○ drew	○ dawn	● royal
7. renew	● stew	○ coin	○ glow
8. loyal	○ low	○ soil	○ towel
9. employ	○ power	○ join	○ umpire
10. moist	○ jewel	○ just	● joy
11. review	○ choice	○ avoid	● chew
12. threw	○ throw	○ view	○ toy
13. void	● oyster	○ due	○ vendor
14. knew	● crew	○ know	○ annoy

Page 54 — To Grandmother's House

A **compound** word is formed when two independent words come together.

Example: My father just bought a new **lawnmower**.

Directions: Find the path to Grandmother's house by coloring each stepping stone brown that contains a compound word.

Page 55 — Contractions

Contractions are shortened forms of two words. We use apostrophes to show where letters are missing.

Example: It is = it's

Directions: Write the words that are used in each contraction.

- we're = **we** + **are**
- they'll = **they** + **will**
- you'll = **you** + **will**
- aren't = **are** + **not**
- I'm = **I** + **am**
- isn't = **is** + **not**

Directions: Write the contraction for the two words shown.

- you have — **you've**
- have not — **haven't**
- had not — **hadn't**
- we will — **we'll**
- they are — **they're**
- he is — **he's**
- she had — **she'd**
- it will — **it'll**
- I am — **I'm**
- is not — **isn't**

Page 56 — Capitalization and Commas

We **capitalize** the names of cities and states. We use a **comma** to separate the name of a city and a state.

Directions: Use capital letters and commas to write the names of the cities and states correctly.

Example: sioux falls south dakota — **Sioux Falls, South Dakota**

1. plymouth massachusetts — **Plymouth, Massachusetts**
2. boston massachusetts — **Boston, Massachusetts**
3. philadelphia pennsylvania — **Philadelphia, Pennsylvania**
4. white plains new york — **White Plains, New York**
5. newport rhode island — **Newport, Rhode Island**
6. yorktown virginia — **Yorktown, Virginia**
7. nashville tennessee — **Nashville, Tennessee**
8. portland oregon — **Portland, Oregon**
9. mansfield ohio — **Mansfield, Ohio**

Page 57 — Perfectly Punctuated

A statement ends with a period. (.)
A question ends with a question mark. (?)
An exclamation ends with an exclamation mark. (!)

Directions: Write the correct punctuation mark in each box.

1. Every Saturday morning we help a senior citizen [.]
2. Would you like to help us this Saturday [?]
3. You can help me gather the supplies we will need [.]
4. Today we are raking Mrs. Ray's yard [.]
5. That elm tree is huge [!]
6. Will you help them rake the backyard [?]
7. Don't mow too close to the flowers [.]
8. Mrs. Ray has left lemonade there for us [.]
9. I will mow the front yard [.]
10. Will you sweep the front walks [?]
11. She thinks the yard looks super [!]
12. What will we do next Saturday [?]

Page 58 — You Name It!

Nouns are words that tell the names of people, places, or things.

Directions: Write nouns that name people.
Directions: Write nouns that name places.
Directions: Write nouns that name things.

Answers will vary.

91

Summer Success

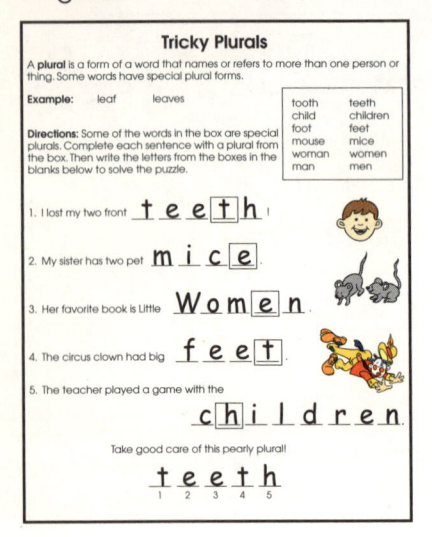

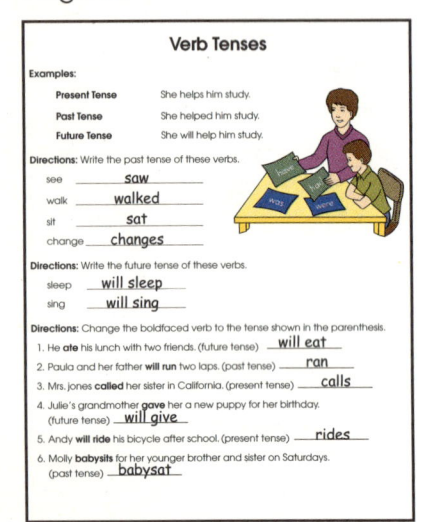

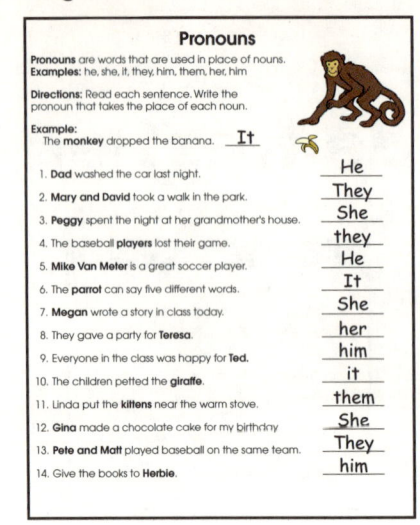

Page 59 — Tricky Plurals

A **plural** is a form of a word that names or refers to more than one person or thing. Some words have special plural forms.

Example: leaf → leaves

Box: tooth / teeth, child / children, foot / feet, mouse / mice, woman / women, man / men

Directions: Some of the words in the box are special plurals. Complete each sentence with a plural from the box. Then write the letters from the boxes in the blanks below to solve the puzzle.

1. I lost my two front **teeth**.
2. My sister has two pet **mice**.
3. Her favorite book is Little **Women**.
4. The circus clown had big **feet**.
5. The teacher played a game with the **children**.

Take good care of this pearly plural!

teeth (1 2 3 4 5)

Page 60 — Pronouns

Pronouns are words that are used in place of nouns.
Examples: he, she, it, they, him, them, her, him

Directions: Read each sentence. Write the pronoun that takes the place of each noun.

Example: The **monkey** dropped the banana. **It**

1. **Dad** washed the car last night. — He
2. **Mary and David** took a walk in the park. — They
3. **Peggy** spent the night at her grandmother's house. — She
4. The baseball **players** lost their game. — they
5. **Mike Van Meter** is a great soccer player. — He
6. The **parrot** can say five different words. — It
7. **Megan** wrote a story in class today. — She
8. They gave a party for **Teresa**. — her
9. Everyone in the class was happy for **Ted**. — him
10. The children petted the **giraffe**. — it
11. Linda put the **kittens** near the warm stove. — them
12. **Gina** made a chocolate cake for my birthday. — She
13. **Pete and Matt** played baseball on the same team. — They
14. Give the books to **Herbie**. — him

Page 61 — Smooth Sailing

A **verb** is a word that can show action. A verb can also tell what someone or something is or is like.

Examples: The boats **sail** on Lake Michigan. We **eat** dinner at 6:00. I **am** ten years old. The clowns **were** funny.

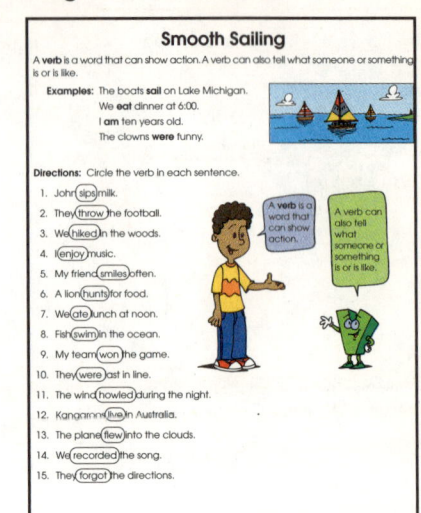

Directions: Circle the verb in each sentence.

1. John (sips) milk.
2. They (throw) the football.
3. We (hiked) in the woods.
4. I (enjoy) music.
5. My friend (smiles) often.
6. A lion (hunts) for food.
7. We (ate) lunch at noon.
8. Fish (swim) in the ocean.
9. My team (won) the game.
10. They (were) last in line.
11. The wind (howled) during the night.
12. Kangaroos (live) in Australia.
13. The plane (flew) into the clouds.
14. We (recorded) the song.
15. They (forgot) the directions.

Page 62 — Verb Tenses

Examples:
- Present Tense: She helps him study.
- Past Tense: She helped him study.
- Future Tense: She will help him study.

Directions: Write the past tense of these verbs.
- see — saw
- walk — walked
- sit — sat
- change — changed

Directions: Write the future tense of these verbs.
- sleep — will sleep
- sing — will sing

Directions: Change the boldfaced verb to the tense shown in the parenthesis.

1. He **ate** his lunch with two friends. (future tense) — will eat
2. Paula and her father **will run** two laps. (past tense) — ran
3. Mrs. Jones **called** her sister in California. (present tense) — calls
4. Julie's grandmother **gave** her a new puppy for her birthday. (future tense) — will give
5. Andy **will ride** his bicycle after school. (present tense) — rides
6. Molly **babysits** for her younger brother and sister on Saturdays. (past tense) — babysat

Page 63 — Awesome Adjectives

Adjectives tell more about nouns. Adjectives are describing words.
Examples: **scary** animals, **bright** glow, **wet** frog

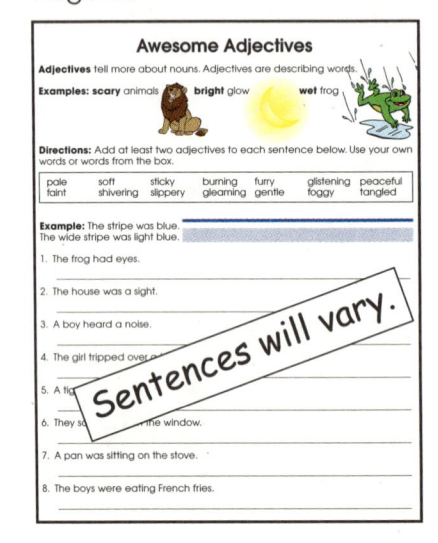

Directions: Add at least two adjectives to each sentence below. Use your own words or words from the box.

Box: pale, soft, sticky, burning, furry, glistening, peaceful, faint, shivering, slippery, gleaming, gentle, foggy, tangled

Example: The stripe was blue. → The wide stripe was light blue.

1. The frog had eyes.
2. The house was a sight.
3. A boy heard a noise.
4. The girl tripped over...
5. A tiger...
6. They saw... the window.
7. A pan was sitting on the stove.
8. The boys were eating French fries.

Sentences will vary.

Page 64 — Adverbs Away!

Adverbs tell when, where, or how about the verb in a sentence. Many adverbs end in **ly** when answering the question, "How?"

Examples: I celebrated my birthday **today**. (When?) Children sat **near** me. (Where?) I **excitedly** opened my gifts. (How?)

Directions: Underline the adverb in each sentence. Then, write **when**, **where** or **how** on the line to tell which question it answers.

1. The children played quietly at home. — how
2. We went to the movie yesterday. — when
3. My friends came inside to play. — where
4. The child cut his meat carefully. — how
5. The girls ran upstairs to get their coats. — where
6. The play-off games start tomorrow. — when
7. The boys walked slowly. — how
8. The teacher said, "Write your name neatly." — how

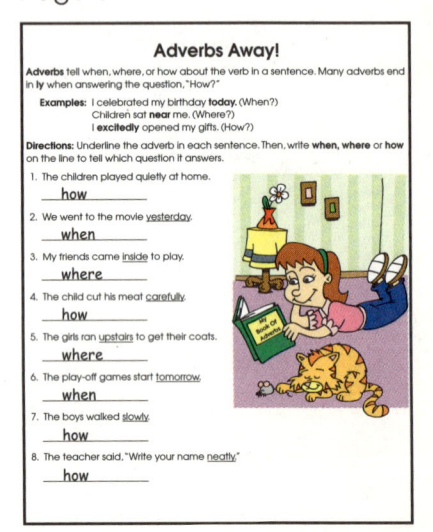

Page 65 — Classifying

Directions: Read the story. Find words in the story that belong in the lists below. Write the words under the correct lists.

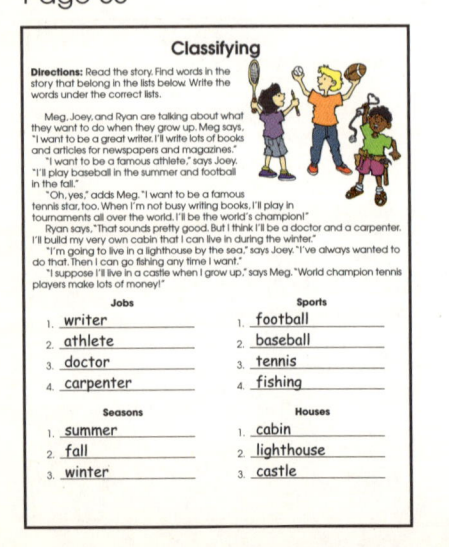

Meg, Joey, and Ryan are talking about what they want to do when they grow up. Meg says, "I want to be a great writer. I'll write lots of books and articles for newspapers and magazines."

"Oh, yes," adds Meg. "I want to be a famous tennis star, too. When I'm not busy writing books, I'll play in tournaments all over the world. I'll be the world's champion!"

Ryan says, "That sounds pretty good. But I think I'll be a doctor and a carpenter. I'll build my very own cabin that I can live in during the winter."

"I'm going to live in a lighthouse by the sea," says Joey. "I've always wanted to do that. Then I can go fishing any time I want."

"I suppose I'll live in a castle when I grow up," says Meg. "World champion tennis players make lots of money!"

Jobs
1. writer
2. athlete
3. doctor
4. carpenter

Sports
1. football
2. baseball
3. tennis
4. fishing

Seasons
1. summer
2. fall
3. winter

Houses
1. cabin
2. lighthouse
3. castle

Page 66 — The Maya Indians

The **main idea** is sometimes stated in one of the sentences of a paragraph. Other sentences in the paragraph give more information about the main idea. These other bits of information are called **supporting details**.

Directions: Read the paragraphs and answer the questions.

Mayan scholars made cultural advances in astronomy and mathematics. They studied the Moon and the planets. They also made accurate records and predictions of their cycles. They developed two calendars. One calendar predicted good or bad luck. The second calendar, like ours, had 365 days. The Mayans had a number system that consisted of dots and bars. The Mayans were probably the first people to use the concept of zero.

1. What is the main idea? — Mayan scholars made cultural advances in astronomy and mathematics.
2. What are two details that support the main idea? — Answers will vary but may include: They studied the moon and the planets. The Indians had a number system that consisted of dots and bars.

The Mayan heritage continues with many people of Mexico and Central America. More than 20 languages and dialects are said to have developed from the ancient Mayan language. Many of their descendants still carry on some of the traditional religious customs. Also, the ruins of ancient Mayan cities are visited each year by many tourists.

3. What is the main idea? — The Mayan heritage continues with many people of Mexico and Central America.
4. What are two details that support the main idea? — Answers will vary. More than 20 languages have developed from the ancient Mayan language. Descendants still carry on some of the traditional religious customs.

Page 67 — Benjamin Franklin

Benjamin Franklin was born in Boston, Massachusetts, on January 17, 1706. Even though he only attended school to age 10, he worked hard to improve his mind and character. He taught himself several foreign languages and learned much that would later be a great help to him. Ben Franklin played a very important part in our history. One of his many accomplishments was as a printer. He was a helper (apprentice) to his half-brother, James, and later moved to the city of Philadelphia where he worked in another print shop.

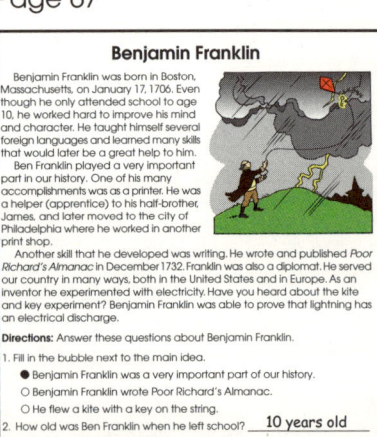

Another skill that he developed was writing. He wrote and published *Poor Richard's Almanac* in December 1732. Franklin was also a diplomat. He served our country in many ways, both in the United States and in Europe. As an inventor he experimented with electricity. Have you heard about the kite and key experiment? Benjamin Franklin was able to prove that lightning has an electrical discharge.

Directions: Answer these questions about Benjamin Franklin.

1. Fill in the bubble next to the main idea.
   - ● Benjamin Franklin was a very important part of our history.
   - ○ Benjamin Franklin wrote Poor Richard's Almanac.
   - ○ He flew a kite with a key on the string.
2. How old was Ben Franklin when he left school? — 10 years old
3. Write three of Ben Franklin's accomplishments.
   1) He wrote Poor Richards Almanac.
   2) He was a diplomat.
   3) He proved lightning has an electrical discharge.

Summer Success

Page 68

Crater Lake

When you come to a word you don't know, look for clues to its meaning in the words around it. These nearby words are called **context clues** and can help you figure out a new word.

Example: Mount Mazama, an ancient volcano, collapsed thousands of years ago, leaving a huge bowl, or crater.
Context Clues: thousands, years ago
Meaning: very old

Directions: Fill in the bubble next to the correct meaning of the underlined word.

1. Crater Lake, in the Cascade Mountains of southern Oregon, rests in an inactive volcano at an altitude of about 6,200 feet above sea level.
   - ○ height   ○ average
2. No streams or rivers supply the lake with water. Precipitation, in the form of snow and rain, has filled the crater.
   - ● fill   ○ save
3. Crater Lake is the deepest lake in the United States. It is 1,932 feet at its greatest depth.
   - ○ far   ● measurement downward
4. Years ago, a mining prospector was looking for minerals and oil. He saw the lake and called it "Deep Blue Lake" because of its beautiful color.
   - ● explorer   ○ beautiful
5. Crater Lake and the area around it are now part of a National Park. The Park Service will ensure people do not pollute the lake.
   - ○ protect   ● make certain
6. There were no fish in Crater Lake until it was stocked with trout in 1888. People who fish are happy that more fish are still added each year.
   - ○ stored   ● filled

Page 69

How Plants Get Food

Every living thing needs food. Did you ever wonder how plants get food? They do not sit down and eat a bowl of soup! Plants get their food from the soil and from water. To see how, cut off some stalks of celery. Put the stalks in a clear glass. Fill the glass half full of water. Add a few drops of red food coloring to the water. Leave it overnight. The next day you will see that parts of the celery have turned red! The red lines show how the celery "sucked up" water.

Directions: Answer these questions about how plants get food.

1. Name two ways plants get food.
   1) from soil
   2) from water

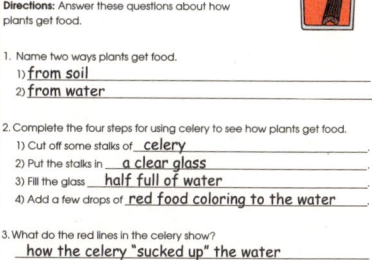

2. Complete the four steps for using celery to see how plants get food.
   1) Cut off some stalks of celery
   2) Put the stalks in a clear glass
   3) Fill the glass half full of water
   4) Add a few drops of red food coloring to the water

3. What do the red lines in the celery show?
   how the celery "sucked up" the water

Page 70

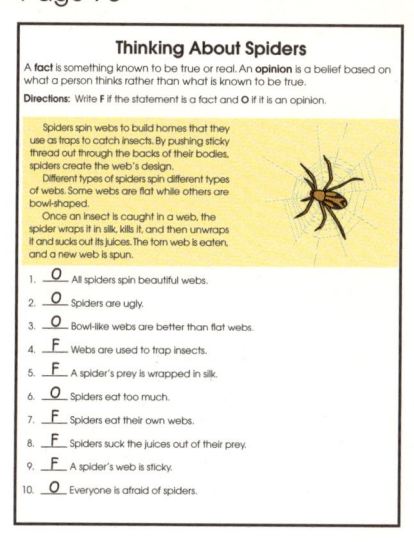

Thinking About Spiders

A **fact** is something known to be true or real. An **opinion** is a belief based on what a person thinks rather than what is known to be true.

Directions: Write F if the statement is a fact and O if it is an opinion.

Spiders spin webs to build homes that they use as traps to catch insects. By pushing sticky thread out through the backs of their bodies, spiders create the web's design.
Different types of spiders spin different types of webs. Some webs are flat while others are bowl-shaped.
Once an insect is caught in a web, the spider wraps it in silk, kills it, and then unwraps it and sucks out its juices. The torn web is eaten, and a new web is spun.

1. O All spiders spin beautiful webs.
2. O Spiders are ugly.
3. O Bowl-like webs are better than flat webs.
4. F Webs are used to trap insects.
5. F A spider's prey is wrapped in silk.
6. O Spiders eat too much.
7. F Spiders eat their own webs.
8. F Spiders suck the juices out of their prey.
9. F A spider's web is sticky.
10. O Everyone is afraid of spiders.

Page 71

Compare and Contrast

Directions: Look for similarities and differences in the following paragraphs. Then answer the questions.

Phong and Chris both live in the city. They live in the same apartment building and go to the same school. Phong and Chris sometimes walk to school together. If it is raining or storming, Phong's dad drives them to school on his way to work. In the summer, they spend a lot of time at the park across the street from their building.

Phong lives in Apartment 12-A with his little sister and mom and dad. He has a collection of model race cars that he put together with his dad's help. He even has a bookshelf full of books about race cars and race car drivers.

Chris has a big family. He has two older brothers and one older sister. When Chris has time to do anything he wants, he gets out his butterfly collection. He notes the place he found each specimen and the day he found it. He also likes to play with puzzles.

1. Compare Phong and Chris. List at least three similarities.
   They both live in the city.
   Phong and Chris spend a lot of time at the park.
   They go to the same school.

2. Contrast Phong and Chris. List two differences.
   Phong has a little sister; Chris has two brothers and one sister. Chris has a butterfly collection; Phong collects model race cars.

Page 72

Drawing Conclusions

Drawing a conclusion means to use clues to make a final decision about something. To draw a conclusion, you must read carefully.

Directions: Read each story carefully. Use the clues given to draw a conclusion about the story.

The boy and girl took turns pushing the shopping cart. They went up and down the aisles. Each time they stopped the cart, they would look at things on the shelf and decide what they needed. Jody asked her older brother, "Will I need a box of 48 crayons in Mrs. Charles' class?"
"Yes, I think so," he answered. Then he turned to their mother and said, "I need some new notebooks. Can I get some?"

1. Where are they? at the store
2. What are they doing there? buying school supplies
3. How do you know? Write at least two clue words that helped you.
   Mrs. Charles's class, notebooks, box of 48 crayons

Eric and Randy held on tight. They looked around them and saw that they were not the only ones holding on. The car moved slowly upward. As they turned and looked over the side, they noticed that the people far below them seemed to be getting smaller and smaller. "Hey, Eric, did I tell you this is my first time on one of these?" asked Randy. As they started down the hill at a frightening speed, Randy screamed, "And it may be my last!"

1. Where are they? on a roller coaster
2. How do you know? Write at least two clue words that helped you.
   car moved slowly upward, down at frightening speed

Page 73

Cause and Effect

Cause and effect sentences often use clue words to show the relationship between two events. Common clue words are *because, so, when,* and *since*.

Directions: Read the sentences and circle each clue word. The first one has been done for you.

1. I'll help you clean your room, (so) we can go out to play sooner.
2. (Because) of the heavy snowfall, school was closed today.
3. She was not smiling, (so) her mother wanted her school pictures taken again.
4. Mrs. Wilderman came to school with crutches today (because) she had a skating accident.
5. (When) the team began making too many mistakes at practice, the coach told them to take a break.

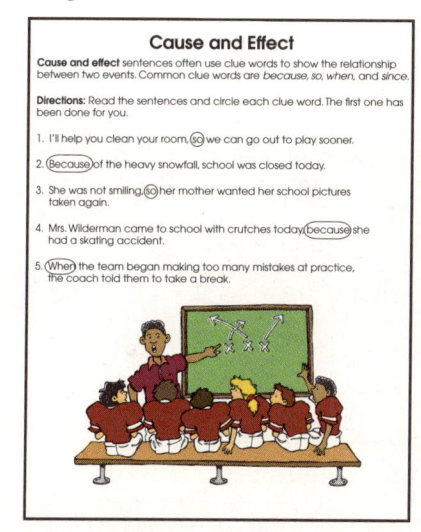

Page 74

Which Way Down?

Thinking about what might happen next is called **predicting outcomes**.

Directions: Read the story. Then, write a word from the box to complete each sentence.

Maria and her family enjoy going to Water Slide Park on Saturdays because there are so many fun things to do. Maria's older sister and brother like to go down Daredevil Slide. Maria usually goes down Lazy Falls Slide because it isn't as steep.
One Saturday, Maria's sister and brother talk her into climbing up Daredevil Slide. They tell her how much fun it is. The lifeguard assures Maria it's safe and promises to watch her. Maria looks down at Daredevil Slide. Then, she looks over at Lazy Falls Slide. Maria feels very brave.

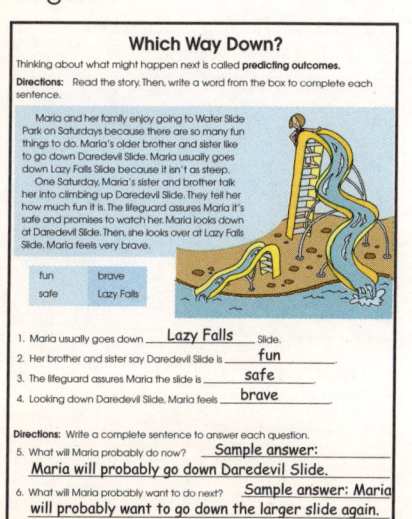

| fun | brave |
| safe | Lazy Falls |

1. Maria usually goes down Lazy Falls Slide.
2. Her brother and sister say Daredevil Slide is fun.
3. The lifeguard assures Maria the slide is safe.
4. Looking down Daredevil Slide, Maria feels brave.

Directions: Write a complete sentence to answer each question.

5. What will Maria probably do now? Sample answer: Maria will probably go down Daredevil Slide.
6. What will Maria probably want to do next? Sample answer: Maria will probably want to go down the larger slide again.

Page 75

What Are You Reading?

A **fiction** book is a book about things that are made up or not true. Fantasy books are fiction. A **nonfiction** book is about things that have really happened. Books can be classified into more types:

Mystery - books that have clues that lead to solving a problem or mystery
Biography - book about a real person's life
Poetry - a collection of poems, which may or may not rhyme
Fantasy - books about things that cannot really happen
Sports - books about different sports or sport figures
Travel - books about going to other places

Directions: Write mystery, biography, poetry, fantasy, sports, or travel next to each title.

The Life of Helen Keller	biography
Let's Go to Mexico!	travel
The Case of the Missing Doll	mystery
How to Play Golf	sports
Turtle Soup and Other Poems	poetry
Fred's Flying Saucer	fantasy

Page 76

Story Elements

A good story will contain these **story elements**:

Title — gives a clue to what the story is about
Setting — tells where and when the story takes place
Characters — describes people in the story
Plot — explains the events in a story that create a problem
Climax — describes the most thrilling part of the story where the problem will either be solved, or it won't
Resolution — tells how the characters solve the story problem
Conclusion — tells what happens to the characters in the end

Directions: Write the letter of the definition that matches the story element.

1. d Setting   a. the way a story ends
2. e Characters   b. the changing point of a story; it is often the most exciting part of the story.
3. c Plot   c. the series of events in a story involving a problem
4. b Climax   d. the place and time
5. f Resolution   e. people or animals in the story
6. a Conclusion   f. the way in which the problems are solved

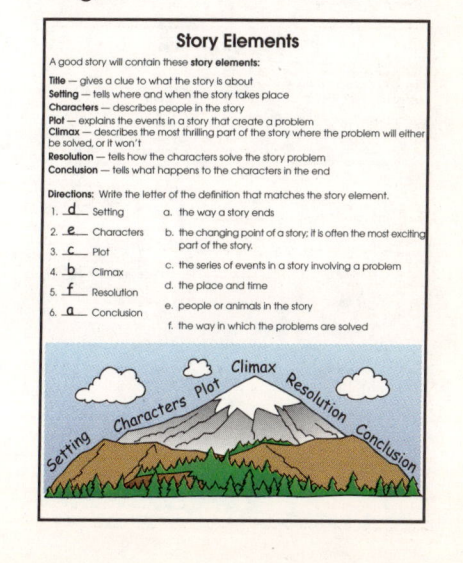

93

Summer Success

Page 77

Story Webs

A **story web** is a way to visually classify a story.
All short stories have a plot, characters, setting, and a theme.
- The **plot** is what the story is about.
- The **characters** are the people or animals in the story.
- The **setting** is where and when the story occurs.
- The **theme** is the message or idea of the story.

Directions: Use the story "Snow White" to complete this story web.

- plot: The wicked stepmother tries to get rid of Snow White.
- characters: Snow White, the seven dwarves, Snow White's stepmother, the Prince
- title of story: "Snow White"
- setting: the palace, the dwarves' cabin in the woods
- theme: Good will triumph over evil.

Page 78

A Series of Wishes

Directions: Read all the sentences. Write the numbers 1–8 in the circles to put the sentences in order. Then, rewrite the sentences in the correct order at the bottom.

- 3 The traveler began to rub the sand off the lantern.
- 7 Second, he wished that he could find his family again.
- 5 The genie said that he would grant the traveler three wishes.
- 1 A traveler had lost his way as he crossed the desert.
- 8 His third wish was that he could have three more wishes.
- 4 As he rubbed the lantern, a genie appeared in a cloud of smoke.
- 2 The lost traveler found an old lantern lying in the sand.
- 6 First, the traveler wished that he would find his way out of the desert.

1. A traveler had lost his way as he crossed the desert.
2. The lost traveler found an old lantern lying in the sand.
3. The traveler began to rub the sand off the lantern.
4. As he rubbed the lantern, a genie appeared in a cloud of smoke.
5. The genie said that he would grant the traveler three wishes.
6. First, the traveler wished that he would find his way out of the desert.
7. Second, he wished that he could find his family again.
8. His third wish was that he could have three more wishes.

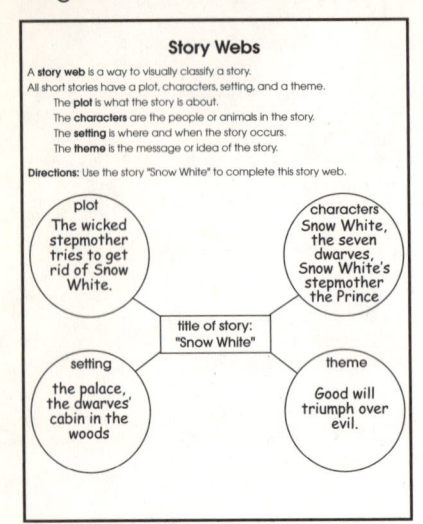

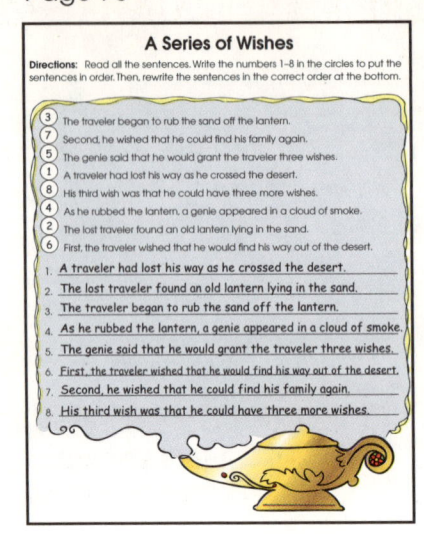

Page 79

Organize Your Thoughts

An **autobiography** is a written account of your life. An outline can help you to organize details about your life.

Directions: Fill in the outline with information about your life.

I. My Early Years
  A. Birthdate _____ Place _____
  B. Favorite activities _____
  C. Family members _____
  D. Things I learned _____
  E. First school _____
II. My Present
  A. School grade _____
  B. Friends _____
  C. Favorite subjects _____
  D. Sports or hobbies _____
  E. Family fun _____
III. My Future
  A. Middle School/High School _____
  B. College _____
  C. Ambitions _____
  D. Places I would like to see _____
  E. Things I would like to accomplish _____

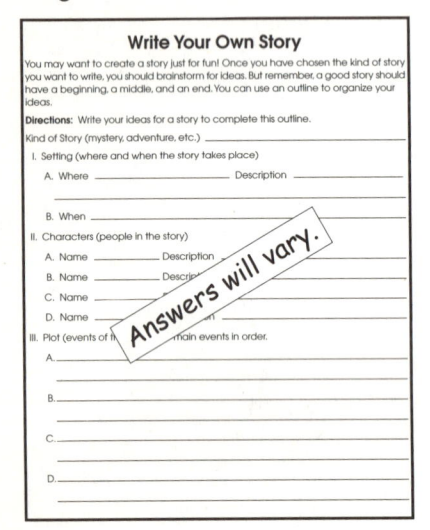

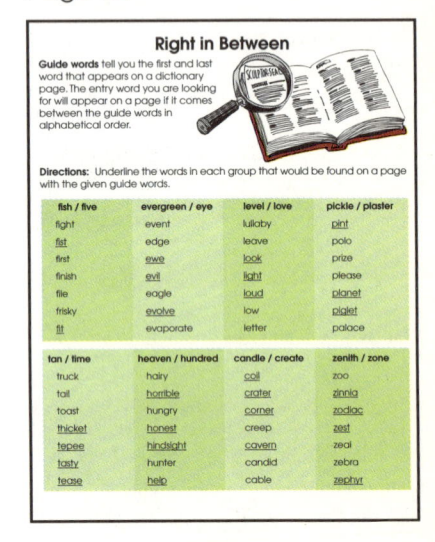

Answers will vary.

Page 80

Write Your Own Story

You may want to create a story just for fun! Once you have chosen the kind of story you want to write, you should brainstorm for ideas. But remember, a good story should have a beginning, a middle, and an end. You can use an outline to organize your ideas.

Directions: Write your ideas for a story to complete this outline.

Kind of Story (mystery, adventure, etc.) _____

I. Setting (where and when the story takes place)
  A. Where _____ Description _____
  B. When _____
II. Characters (people in the story)
  A. Name _____ Description _____
  B. Name _____ Description _____
  C. Name _____
  D. Name _____
III. Plot (events of the story—main events in order)
  A. _____
  B. _____
  C. _____
  D. _____

Answers will vary.

Page 81

Dictionary Mystery

Directions: Below are six dictionary entries with pronunciations and definitions. The only things missing are the entry words. Write the correct entry words. Be sure to spell each word correctly.

Entry word: **rose** (rōz) — A flower that grows on bushes and vines.

Entry word: **rabbit** (ra bet) — A small animal that has long ears.

Entry word: **fox** (fŏks) — A wild animal that lives in the woods.

Entry word: **piano** (pē an ō) — A musical instrument that has many keys.

Entry word: **lake** (lāk) — A body of water that is surrounded by land.

Entry word: **baseball** (bās bôl) — A game played with a bat and a ball.

Directions: Now write the entry words in alphabetical order.

1. baseball
2. fox
3. lake
4. piano
5. rabbit
6. rose

Page 82

Right in Between

Guide words tell you the first and last word that appears on a dictionary page. The entry word you are looking for will appear on a page if it comes between the guide words in alphabetical order.

Directions: Underline the words in each group that would be found on a page with the given guide words.

fish / five	evergreen / eye	level / love	pickle / plaster
fight	event	lullaby	pint
fist	edge	leave	polo
first	**ewe**	look	prize
finish	evil	**light**	please
file	eagle	**loud**	planet
frisky	**evolve**	low	**piglet**
fit	evaporate	letter	palace

tan / time	heaven / hundred	candle / create	zenith / zone
truck	**hairy**	**coil**	zoo
tail	horrible	crater	**zinnia**
toast	hungry	corner	zodiac
thicket	**honest**	creep	**zest**
tepee	**hindsight**	**cavern**	zeal
tasty	hunter	candid	zebra
tease	**help**	cable	**zephyr**

Page 83

Alphabetical Order

The words in these lists begin with the same letter.

Directions: Use the second or third letters of each word to put the lists in alphabetical order.

Example:
- tiger — 3 tiger
- tape — 1 tape
- tide — 2 tide

All three words begin with the same letter (t), so look at the second letters. The letter **a** comes before **i**, so **tape** comes first. Then look at the third letters in **tiger** and **tide** to see which word comes next.

- 3 glad
- 4 goat
- 1 gasoline
- 2 gentle
- 5 grumble

- 3 answer
- 1 about
- 5 ask
- 4 around
- 2 against

- 3 tape
- 4 taste
- 1 table
- 2 talent
- 5 taught

ABC's

94

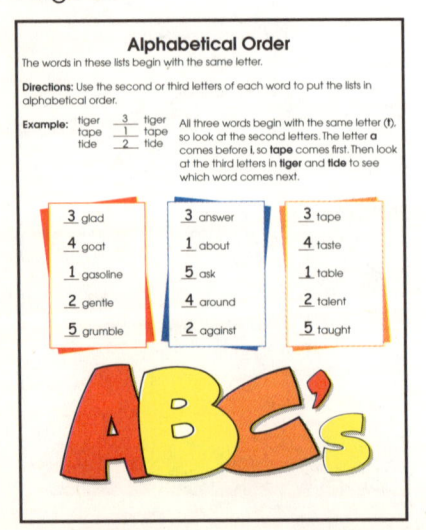

Curriculum Skills for Fourth-Grade Success

McGraw-Hill, the premier education publisher PreK-12, wants to be your partner in helping you educate your child. **Summer Success** was designed to help your child retain those skills learned during the past school year. With **Summer Success**, your child will be ready to review and master new material with confidence when he or she returns to school in the fall.

Use this checklist—compiled from state curriculum standards—to help your child prepare for proficiency testing. Place a check mark in the box if the appropriate skill has been mastered. If your child needs more work with a particular skill, place an "R" in the box and come back to it for review.

Math Skills

- ❑ Understands place value through 999,999.
- ❑ Uses problem-solving strategies—such as rounding, regrouping, using multiple operations, and Venn diagrams—to solve numerical and word problems.
- ❑ Compares whole numbers using < > =.
- ❑ Solves multiple-operation problems using a calculator.
- ❑ Adds and subtracts proper fractions having like denominators of 12 or less.
- ❑ Adds and subtracts simple decimals in context of money with and without regrouping.
- ❑ Tells and writes time shown on traditional and digital clocks.
- ❑ Uses customary system to measure length, mass, volume, and temperature.
- ❑ Uses metric system to measure length, mass, volume, and temperature.
- ❑ Selects the appropriate operational and relational symbols to make an expression true ($4 \times 3 = 12$).
- ❑ Recognizes and uses commutative and associative properties of multiplication ($5 \times 7 = 35$...What is 7×5?).
- ❑ Measures length, width, perimeter, and area to solve numerical and word problems.
- ❑ Describes, draws, identifies, and analyzes two- and three-dimensional shapes.
- ❑ Identifies congruent shapes.
- ❑ Identifies lines of symmetry in shapes.
- ❑ Recognizes patterns and relationships using a bar graph and locating points on a grid.
- ❑ Analyzes and solves simple probability problems.
- ❑ Adds and subtracts with two and three digits, regrouping when necessary
- ❑ Multiplies two-digit numbers with regrouping, and divides one and two-digit numbers by divisors of 6 – 10, with and without remainders.

Summer Success

Language Arts Skills

- ❑ Recognizes and correctly uses parts of speech: nouns, pronouns, verbs, adjectives, adverbs, articles.

- ❑ Understands and correctly uses language conventions: spelling, noun plurals, verb tenses, complete sentences using subject and predicate, contractions, syllables, prefixes, suffixes, base words, idioms.

- ❑ Understands and correctly uses mechanics conventions: capitalization, period, comma, question mark, exclamation point, apostrophe.

- ❑ Uses a variety of vocabulary strategies: synonyms, antonyms, homophones, compound words, affixes, base words, phonics clues, context clues.

- ❑ Understands and correctly uses a variety of writing purposes: letters, lists, poetry, narrative composition, note taking, outlining, webbing.

- ❑ Can locate information in reference materials: table of contents, indexes, glossaries, technology, dictionaries, etc.

Reading Skills

- ❑ Uses reading strategies to understand meaning: sequence, context clues, cause and effect, compare/contrast, classification.

- ❑ Reads for different purposes: main idea, supporting details, following directions, predicting outcomes, making inferences, distinguishing fact/opinion, drawing conclusions.

- ❑ Recognizes story elements: character, setting, plot, conflict, resolution.

- ❑ Distinguishes between fiction and nonfiction.

- ❑ Recognizes a variety of literature forms: biography, poetry, fable, fairytales, historical/science fiction, etc.